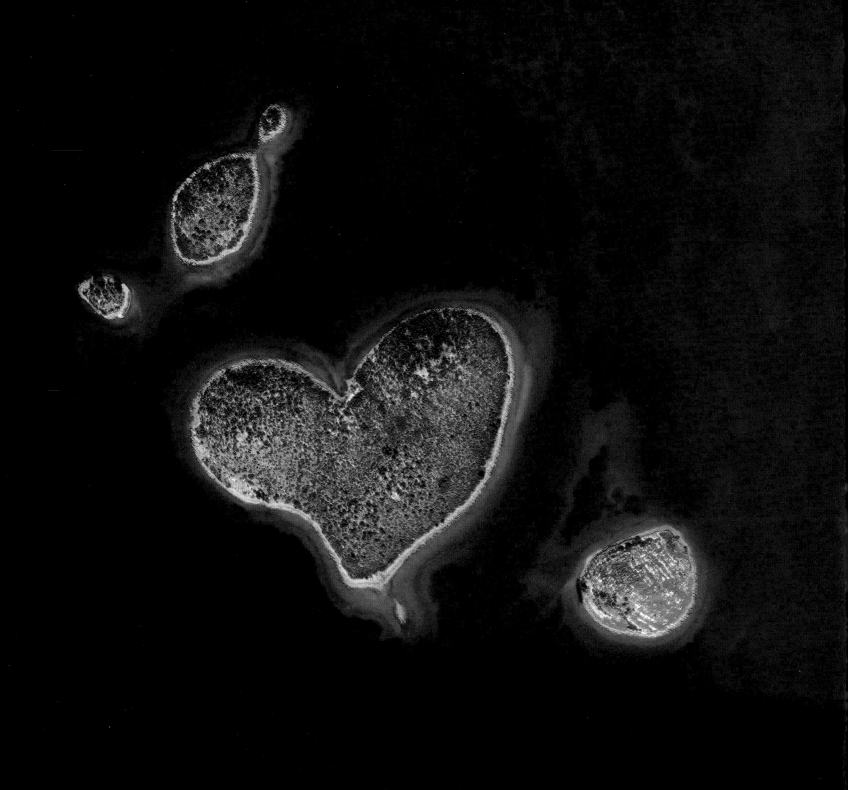

OVERVIEW

YOUNG EXPLORER'S EDITION

A NEW WAY OF SEEING EARTH

BENJAMIN GRANT

with SANDRA MARKLE

Crown Books for Young Readers

New York

To Oma and Opa,
For showing me there is endless wonder to be found on our planet.
And for always encouraging me to go explore it.
—B.G.

For my grandchildren,
because the future belongs to them
—S.M.

CONTENTS

THE OVERVIEW EFFECT

by Scott Kelly, Retired NASA Astronaut

The first time I saw Earth from space, I knew I would never see anything as beautiful. That was in 1999, on my first spaceflight to the Hubble Space Telescope. Since then, I've had the privilege to fly in space three more times. On my most recent mission, I spent an entire year in the International Space Station!

From space, Earth looks like a peaceful place, without political borders. From orbit, astronauts get the sense that this is how Earth was meant to be viewed. This vantage point gives you a sense of oneness, an awareness that we are all part of the same humanity. Many people call this the Overview Effect, which is where this book gets its name. When astronauts experience the Overview Effect, we feel a greater connection to Earth, its people, and the environment that changes us forever.

Exploring the satellite photos in *Overview* allows you to experience some of the beauty and the surprises our planet reveals from above. I hope these spectacular views give you the same sense of connection to Earth that I felt when I was in space.

← **EARTHRISE**

The astronauts of Apollo 8 (1968) were the first humans to leave Earth's orbit. They circled the moon to scout out places where future missions could land. On Christmas Eve, as the spacecraft flew around the dark side of the moon, astronaut Bill Anders took one of the most important photographs of all time—*earthrise*. No human, either in space or on Earth, had ever seen the whole planet like this before, floating like a ball in space—and it changed our view of the planet forever. "It's ironic," Anders remarked later. "We came to discover the moon and we actually discovered Earth."

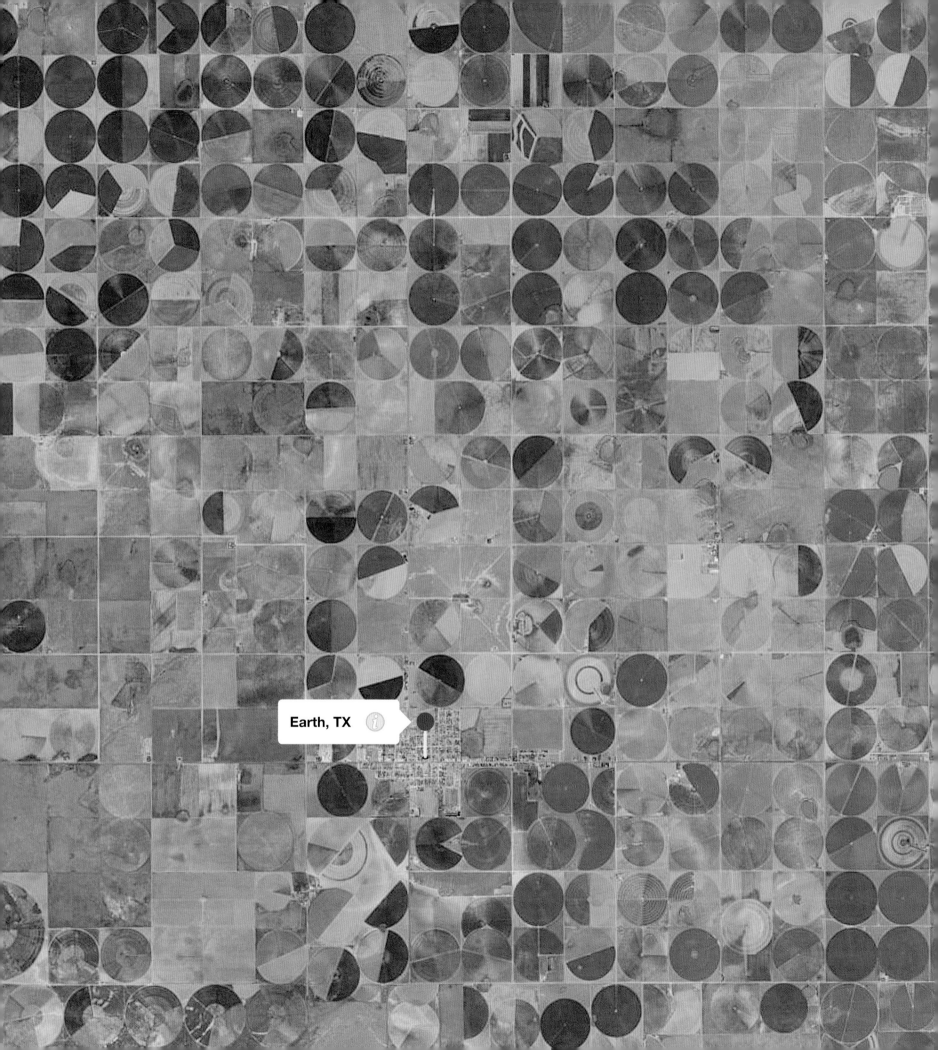

INTRODUCTION

ALWAYS BE EXPLORING

When I was ten years old, my favorite thing to study in school was maps. I am so thankful for my teachers and my parents, who encouraged me to study geography—and all kinds of other topics that fascinated me—with so much passion and joy. Thankfully my parents have never stopped doing this. They helped me understand how important it is to always be exploring.

So it probably won't surprise you that I started a space club at my first office job—where people would come together to discuss the importance of outer space. The idea that sparked Daily Overview, its Instagram page, and this book came from a discovery I made when I was preparing a talk for space club. I wanted to show how satellites affect our daily lives, and while I was exploring this subject, I typed "Earth" into the search bar of a mapping program to see if it would zoom out to show the entire planet. To my surprise, it did the opposite, and zoomed in. The map had indeed settled on Earth—Earth, Texas! I was stunned by what I saw.

These perfect circles filled up my computer screen. Hundreds of them. I had never seen anything like this before. You can see exactly what I discovered in the picture at left. I thought it looked more like something you would see in a modern art museum—coincidentally some of my favorite places in the world to explore.

After a bit of research, I discovered that my entire screen contained pivot irrigation fields— a type of sprinkler system that waters crops in a circular pattern, widely used in the center of the United States. The center of the United States happens to contain Earth, Texas, and that was where this adventure and my passion for this new way of seeing Earth began.

In 2016, I was lucky enough to write and publish *Overview*, the book on which this Young Explorer Edition is based. With the help of children's science writer Sandra Markle, we have adapted the following pages to make it easier for everyone to understand what you are seeing and to experience the Overview Effect.

Above all, I hope this book gives you the chance to look at Earth differently. When we see things in a new way, we are forever changed. With this new perspective comes new understanding. I believe that if we work together and use this knowledge thoughtfully, we will create a better future for our one and only home.

Benjamin Grant

PS: If you want to learn more about the incredible satellite technology that made this book possible, check out page 142.

PART 1

AN AMAZING EARTH

SOSSUSVLEI

Sossusvlei is a desert within Namib-Naukluft National Park in Namibia, the largest conservation area in Africa. The reddish sand dunes found here are among the world's tallest, with many soaring 650 feet (198 m) high. Though winds keep the dunes shifting and the heights changing, the largest dune—nicknamed Big Daddy—averages nearly 1,000 feet (305 m).

CHAPTER 1

A PLANET OF WONDERS

Earth's surface is covered with spectacular features. These places are proof of the amazing power and beauty of nature. Over thousands and thousands of years, many forces on and underneath the planet's surface created the wonders you'll see on the following pages.

Molten lava erupting from deep inside the earth created volcanoes, increasing the amount of land in the process. Tectonic plates beneath the planet's crust slammed together to form immense mountain ranges like the Himalayas, the tallest in the world. Water, gradually breaking down land over billions of years, formed holes like the Grand Canyon. These flowing waterways also created majestic waterfalls like Victoria Falls.

Many of these places are so big, astronauts can see them from space. One of the places they can spot—the Great Barrier Reef off the coast of Australia—was not built by geologic forces; it was created by millions of little coral, growing generation after generation. So in the following pages, enjoy these Overviews that let us see Earth's most wonderful places in a whole new way!

NIAGARA FALLS

Each year, as many as 30 million people visit Niagara Falls, a massive set of waterfalls on the border between the United States and Canada, including the Horseshoe Falls shown in this Overview. During the day, about 757,500 gallons (2,867,449 l) of water thunder over the falls every second! At night, some of the water is channeled into hydroelectric plants to produce enough electricity to power nearly two million homes.

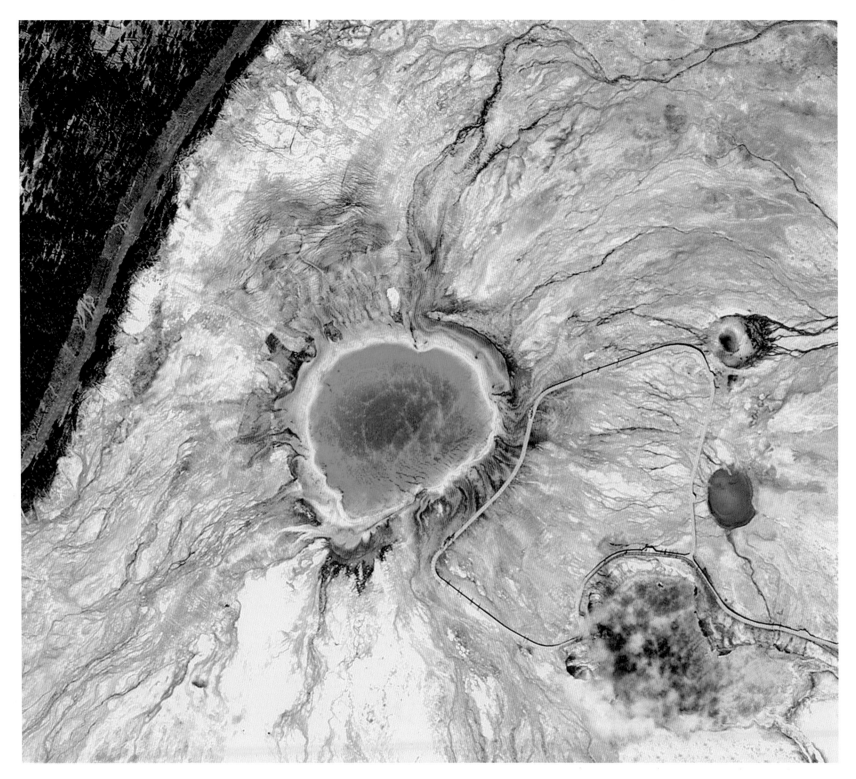

← CRATER LAKE

Crater Lake in Oregon is the deepest lake in the United States and the ninth deepest in the world. A depth of 1,943 feet (592 m) and crystal-clear water give this lake its magnificent blue color. The lake formed inside the collapsed crater from an ancient volcano, so no river feeds into it. Instead, rain and snow restore the water that is lost to evaporation each year.

GRAND PRISMATIC SPRING ↑

The Grand Prismatic Spring is the largest hot spring in Yellowstone National Park, which straddles Wyoming, Montana, and Idaho. The water in the spring is so hot, it would blister your skin. Amazingly, these boiling-hot conditions are perfect for some kinds of microbes (tiny living things). At the center of the spring, where the water is hottest, only a very few microbes can survive, so the water is clear aqua blue. Going out from the center, rings of progressively cooler water are populated by different kinds of microbes, which gives every section a unique color.

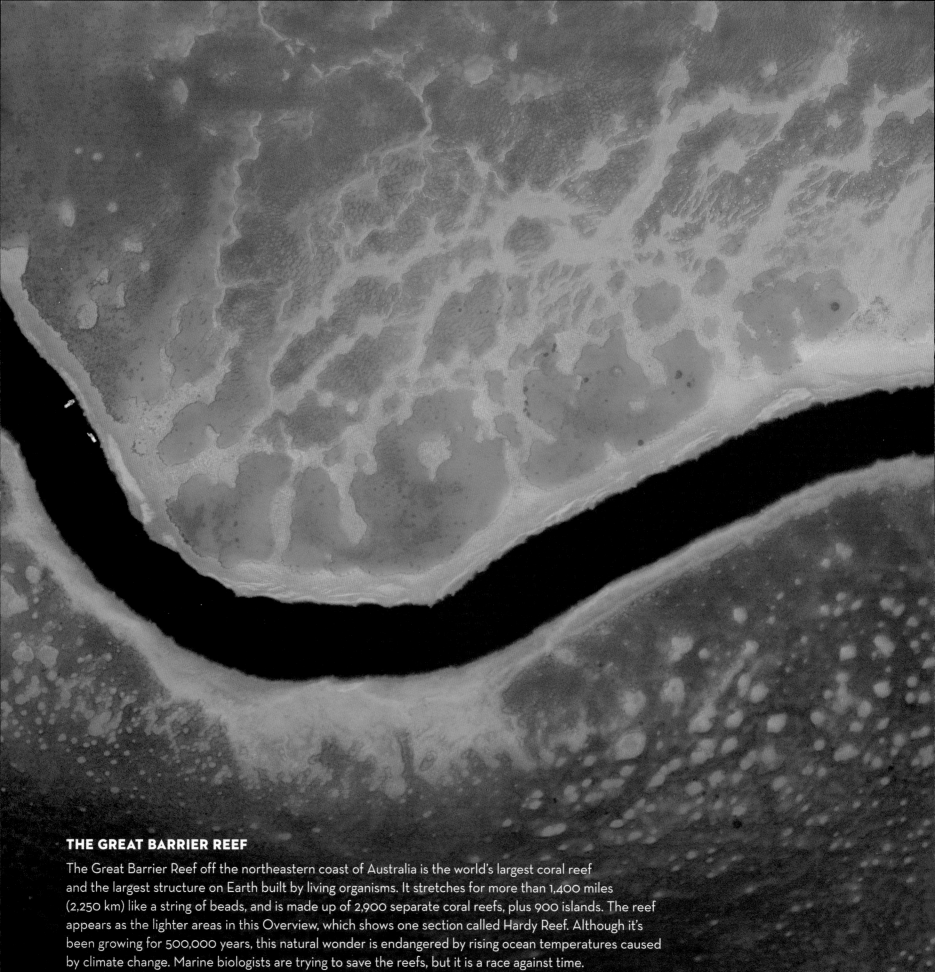

THE GREAT BARRIER REEF

The Great Barrier Reef off the northeastern coast of Australia is the world's largest coral reef and the largest structure on Earth built by living organisms. It stretches for more than 1,400 miles (2,250 km) like a string of beads, and is made up of 2,900 separate coral reefs, plus 900 islands. The reef appears as the lighter areas in this Overview, which shows one section called Hardy Reef. Although it's been growing for 500,000 years, this natural wonder is endangered by rising ocean temperatures caused by climate change. Marine biologists are trying to save the reefs, but it is a race against time.

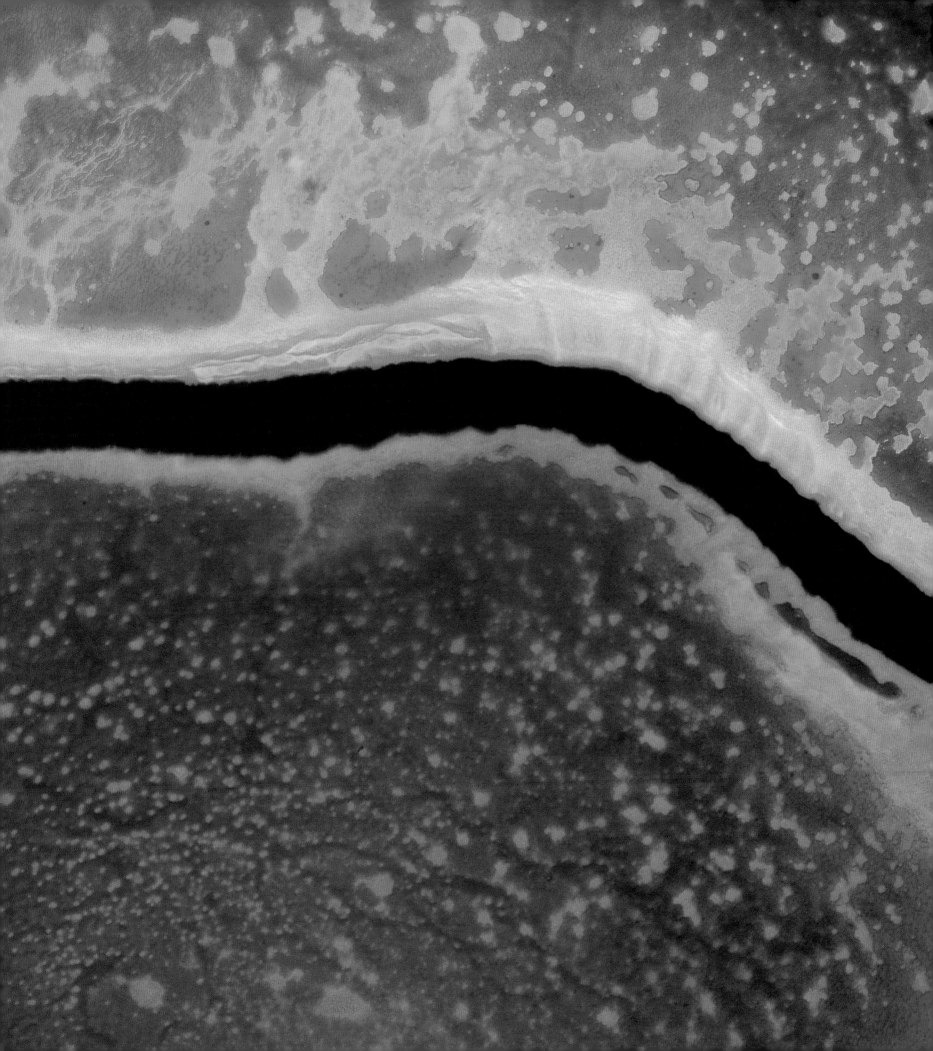

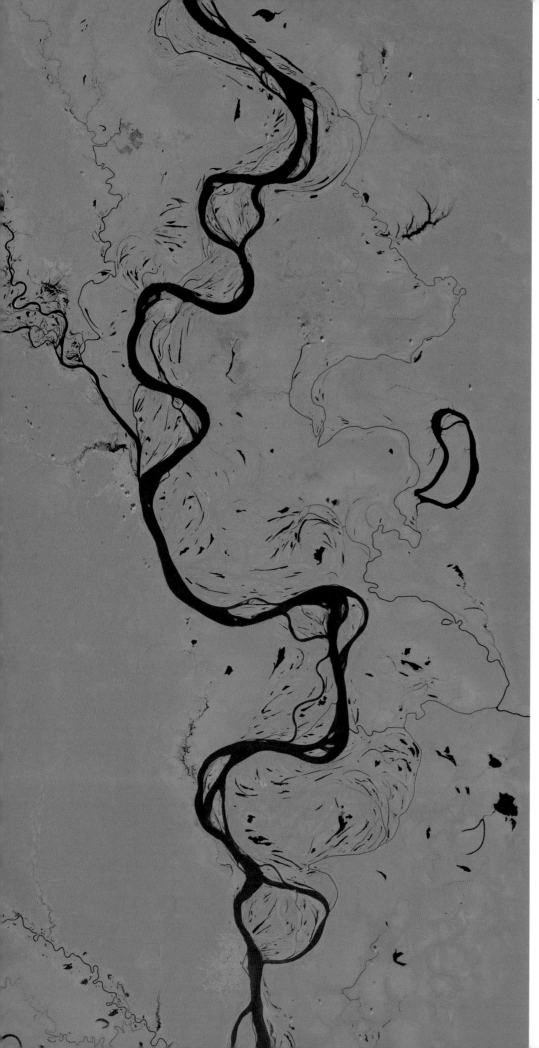

← **AMAZON RIVER**

The Amazon River winds through the rain forests of South America for roughly 4,000 miles (6,400 km). This distance is slightly shorter than the Nile River, the world's longest river. But the Amazon is the world's *largest* river, carrying nearly one-fifth of all the freshwater draining off Earth's surface. In fact, it dumps so much freshwater into the Atlantic Ocean, the Amazon makes the ocean water less salty as far as 100 miles (160 km) from the shore.

VICTORIA FALLS →

With a width of 5,604 feet (1,708 m) and height of 354 feet (108 m), Victoria Falls is the largest waterfall in the world. Located on the border of Zambia and Zimbabwe, the falls are so loud they can be heard from over 20 miles (32 km) away! The spray can be seen for about 30 miles (48 km)! No wonder some locals refer to the falls as the Smoke That Thunders.

THE HIMALAYAS

The Himalyas are the highest mountains in the world, with more than 110 peaks rising as high as 24,000 feet (7,300 m) above sea level. The chain of snowcapped mountains includes the world's tallest, Mount Everest, which peaks at 29,035 feet (8,850 m). Forming the border between Tibet and India, this mountain range extends for 1,500 miles (2,400 km).

(Inset) It's not easy to tell how tall the Himalayas are from directly above, but when you see them from the ground, their towering elevation is impressive!

ULURU

Uluru, also called Ayers Rock, in Australia's Northern Territory, is a giant sandstone rock formation that rises above an otherwise flat plain. Estimated to be 600 million years old, Uluru is 1,142 feet (348 m) high and 6 miles (9.7 km) around at the base. Like a land iceberg, Uluru also extends underground another 2 miles (3.2 km). The rock is a sacred site for the Aboriginal people of the area, who first settled there 10,000 years ago.

MOUNT FUJI

Mount Fuji is Japan's tallest mountain, soaring 12,389 feet (3,776 m) above sea level. It is also an active volcano topped by a crater that is roughly 1,600 feet (488 m) wide. Because it hasn't erupted since 1707—more than 300 years ago—the volcano is classified as "low risk" for erupting. That's good news for the hundreds of thousands of people who hike to the top of Mount Fuji every year!

THE GRAND CANYON

The Grand Canyon in Arizona is one of Earth's most famous wonders. Captured here by a satellite at a low angle, you can see what an amazingly deep gorge it is—averaging 1 mile (1.6 km) deep and 10 miles (16 km) wide. The Grand Canyon was carved by the Colorado River, showcasing water's power to erode a massive amount of rock over time. Scientists have found the oldest rocks at the canyon bottom to be over two billion years old, among the oldest rocks on the planet!

EARTH'S ATMOSPHERE

Earth's atmosphere is a layer of gases—mostly oxygen, nitrogen, and water vapor (water in gas form)—that surrounds the planet, as shown in this photograph taken by an astronaut on board the International Space Station. Every living thing on Earth shares the atmosphere and needs it to survive. Space shuttle astronaut George "Pinky" Nelson once said, "If you draw a circle to represent the Earth, the atmosphere is no thicker than the line you drew." And because it's so thin, even small amounts of smoke from factories and pollutants can have a *big* impact on it.

An aurora is called aurora borealis in the Northern Hemisphere and aurora australis in the Southern Hemisphere, but they are caused by the same thing. Auroras appear when electrically charged atoms from the sun stream through space and smash into the Earth's atmosphere. That collision causes a reaction that gives off light, which cascades through the atmosphere and into our sky. Auroras can occur at any time but are only visible when it's dark—or from space—as is the case for this photograph taken aboard the International Space Station!

CHAPTER 2

A PLANET THAT IS ALIVE

Earth is believed to have formed around 4.5 billion years ago, and like a living thing, it has been changing ever since. Sometimes the impact is sudden, such as when lava erupts to form a volcano. Or when a powerful earthquake drastically shifts and transforms the land. But our planet also changes very slowly as it is carved and shaped by wind and water over time. The winds can pile up massive sand dunes in deserts and continue to shape them every day. Clouds constantly form and break up, playing an important role in the weather and causing the rain that helps plants to grow. Water also changes Earth's surface with the endless power of waves rolling onto shores or the flow of a river carving the land around it.

From outer space, we can see when water in colder places freezes to form the ice of glaciers, which grow and melt over time. Satellite cameras and photographs by astronauts have allowed us to see this connection of natural systems that make Earth feel alive. Whatever forces are at work, our planet's surface is forever a work in progress.

THE EVERGLADES

The Everglades is the largest tropical wilderness in the United States. The national park stretches across 1.5 million acres (607,028 hectares) in Florida. The park was established in 1934 to protect the area's fragile ecosystem. The sediment-filled brown and orange waterways flow through the green mangrove trees. Together, they are home to 36 threatened or protected species, including the American crocodile and manatee.

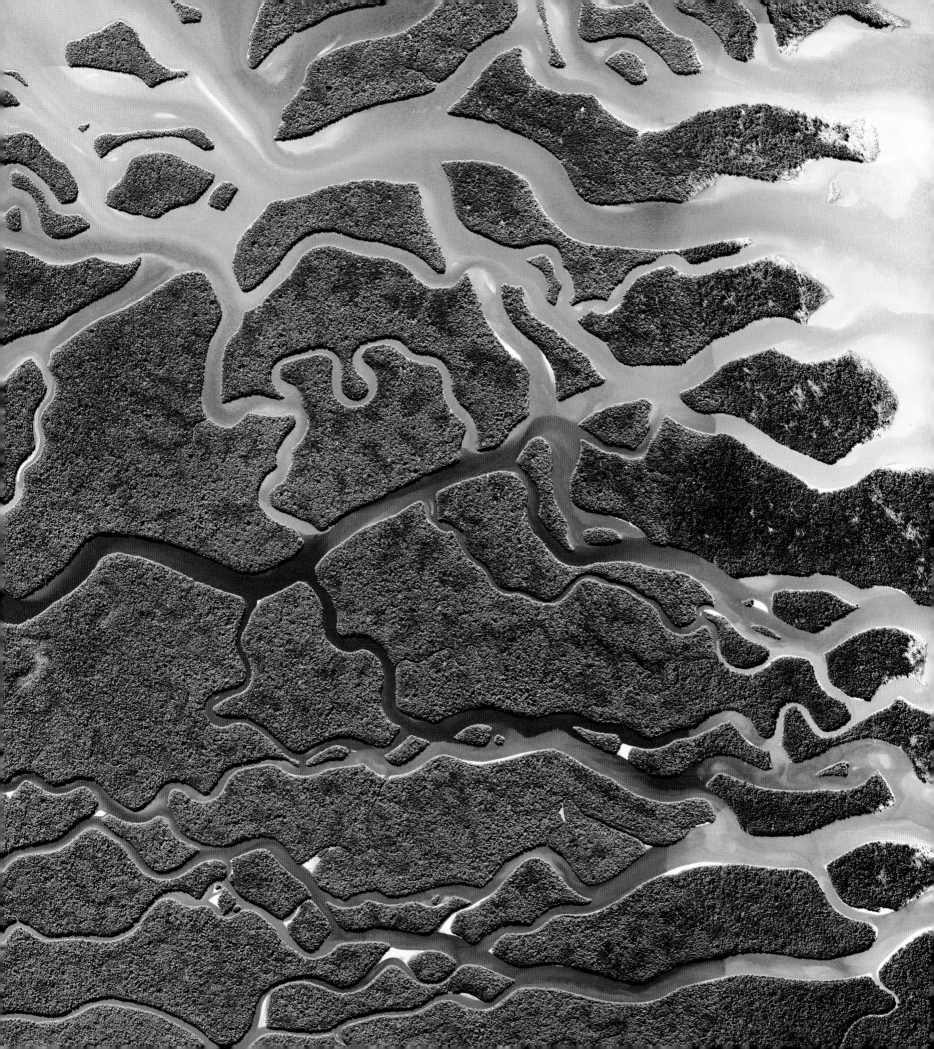

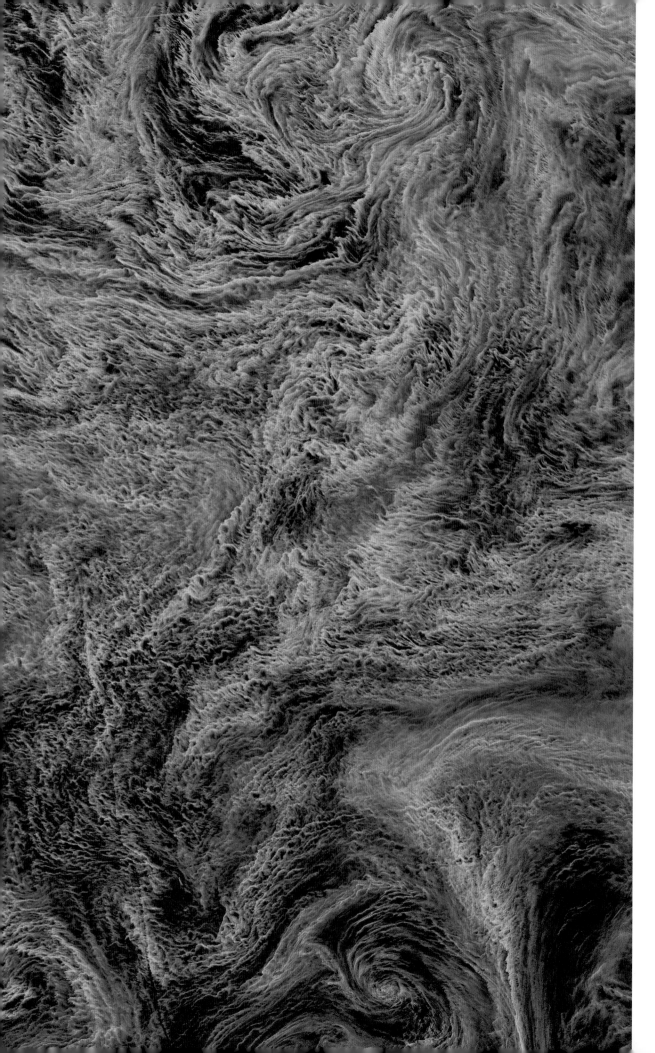

BALTIC ALGAE BLOOM

Whenever there is an excess of nutrients in the water, algae (tiny plants) can grow rapidly, into what is called an algae bloom. It happens around the world in freshwater lakes and oceans. In August 2015, the bloom seen here grew to more than 62 square miles (161 square km) and covered the water in the Baltic Sea. These blue-green algae use up oxygen in the water and can create a "dead zone" for other plants and wildlife.

MONTEVERDE CLOUD FOREST

The Monteverde Cloud Forest grows high up in the Tilarán mountains in Costa Rica. At 4,662 feet (1,421 m) above sea level, Monteverde is very humid, cool, and foggy. These unique conditions make it the perfect home for rare orchids and animals found nowhere else on Earth, such as the raccoon-like olinguito.

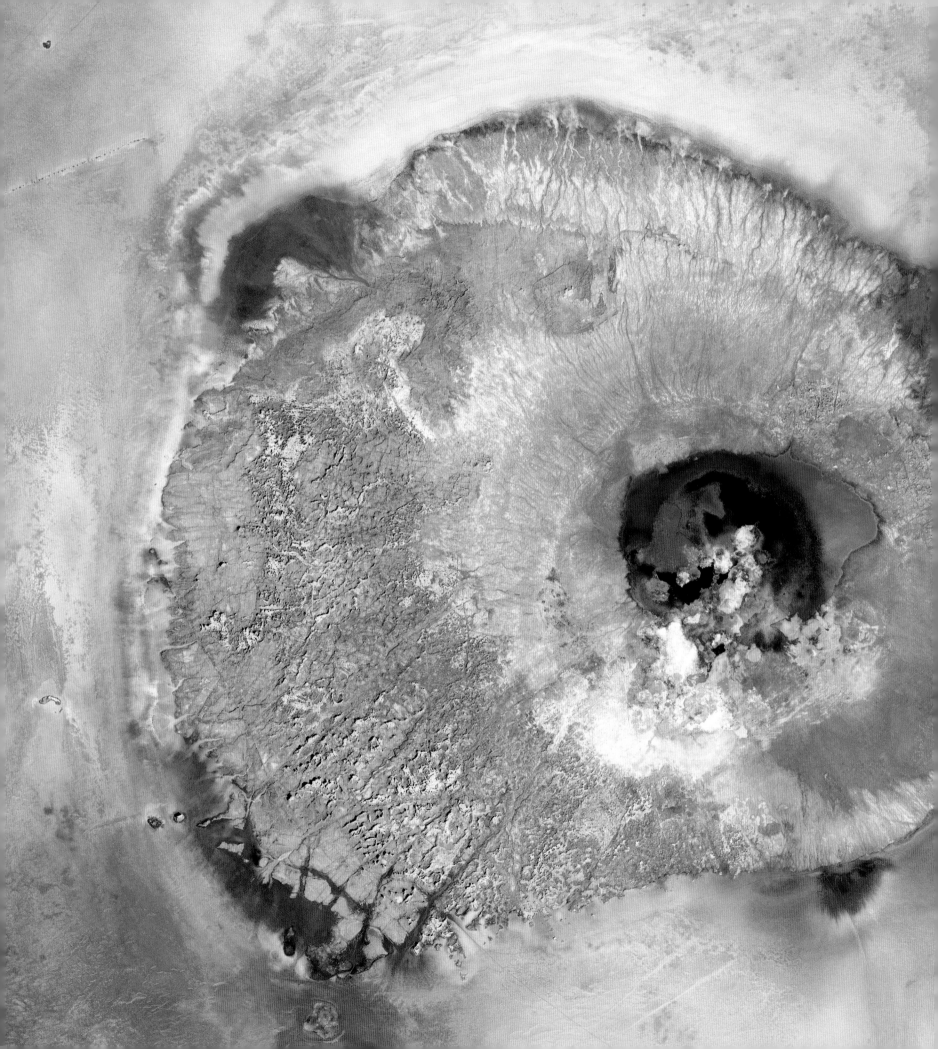

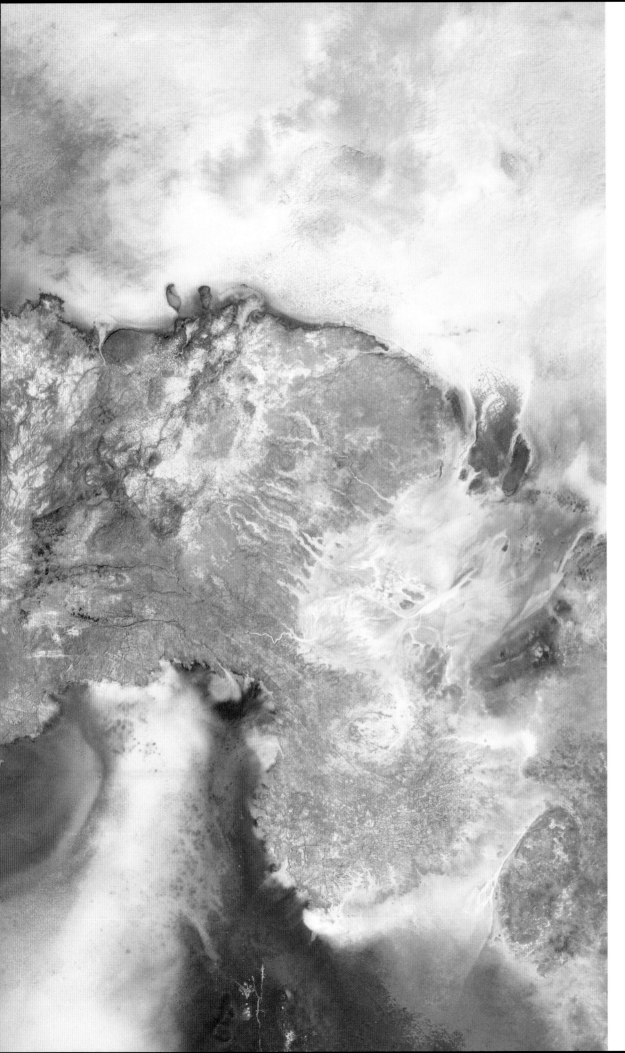

THE DANAKIL DEPRESSION

The Danakil Depression in Ethiopia is one of the lowest places on the planet, located 410 feet (125 m) below sea level. This geologically active area is home to several extreme features—hydrothermal fields, salt pans, volcanoes, and one of Earth's six lava lakes. Even though it is one of the world's hottest places—with temperatures up to 125° Fahrenheit (52° C) and nearly boiling water bubbling up from underground—scientists have discovered extremophiles (tiny organisms able to survive in extreme conditions) living in the water.

NISHINOSHIMA VOLCANO ERUPTION

When the volcano on Nishinoshima, an island southeast of Tokyo, Japan, erupted for two years between November 2013 and November 2015, the island grew in size from 0.02 square miles (0.05 square km) to

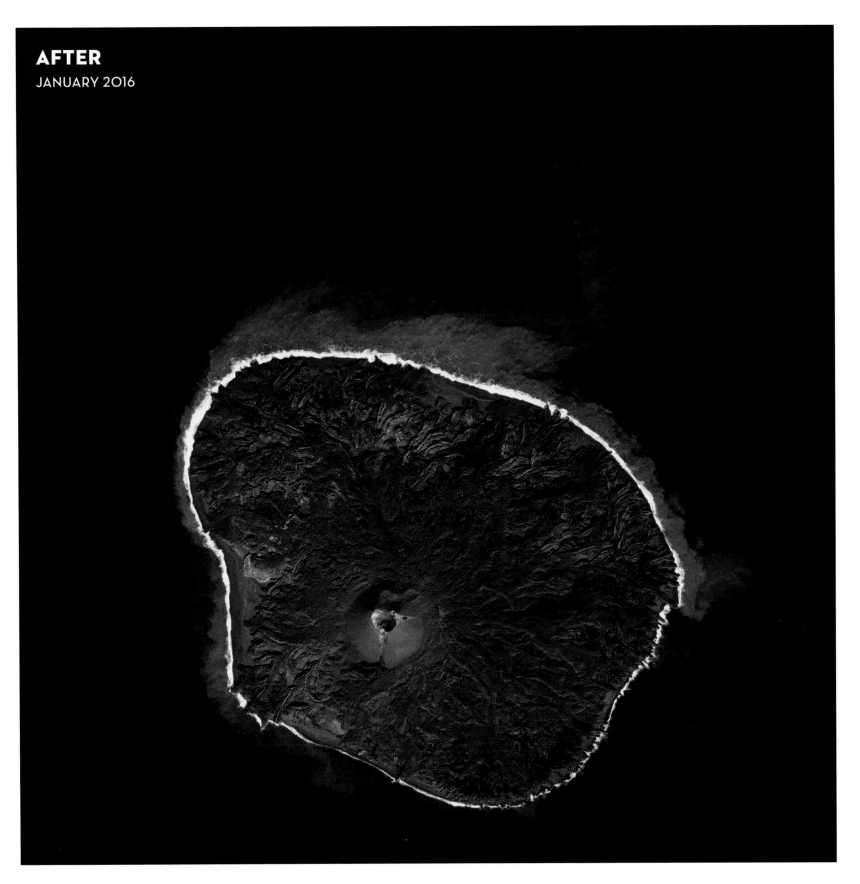

0.89 square miles (2.3 square km)! The During photo shows the island mid-eruption in July 2014, and the After photo shows the enlarged island in January 2016, following the eruption. The volcano erupted again in 2017 and 2018. Clearly, Nishinoshima isn't finished growing!

AUSTRALIAN WAVES

The beaches in Perth, Australia, are world-famous for their beautiful white sand and clear blue water. When seen from above, we also discover the currents and swirls that are created here when waves hit offshore reefs. While the patterns in the water may be beautiful, they create powerful undertows that are dangerous for surfers and swimmers.

ICELAND GLACIER MELT

The sediment-loaded floodwater of the Skaftá River in Iceland creates amazing braided streams and markings on the land as it flows around rocks and down hillsides on its way to the Atlantic Ocean. Hot lava, steam vents, and newly opened hot springs melt the glaciers in the area, causing a large release of water that from space appears as these beautiful patterns.

THE EMPTY QUARTER

The Empty Quarter is the world's largest stretch of sand. It covers parts of Saudi Arabia, Oman, Yemen, and the United Arab Emirates. Roughly 250,000 square miles (648,000 square km), it's just a little smaller than Texas. The raised, hardened formations were sites of shallow lakes thousands of years ago, but not much lives there now since this area gets less than 1.4 inches (35 mm) of rain per year!

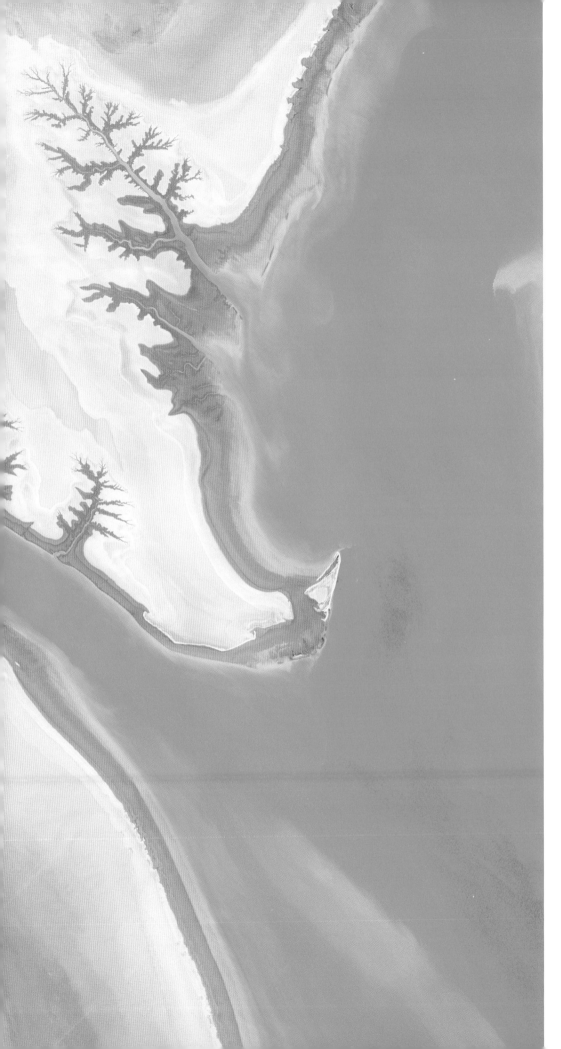

SHADEGAN LAGOON

From space, it is easy to see how water flowing across the land has shaped it. What looks like trees (or a brain!) is actually the water draining from the Shadegan Lagoon into Musa Bay in Iran. Sadly, this wetland area is now frequently contaminated by oil leaking from pipes and fertilizers draining from farmland.

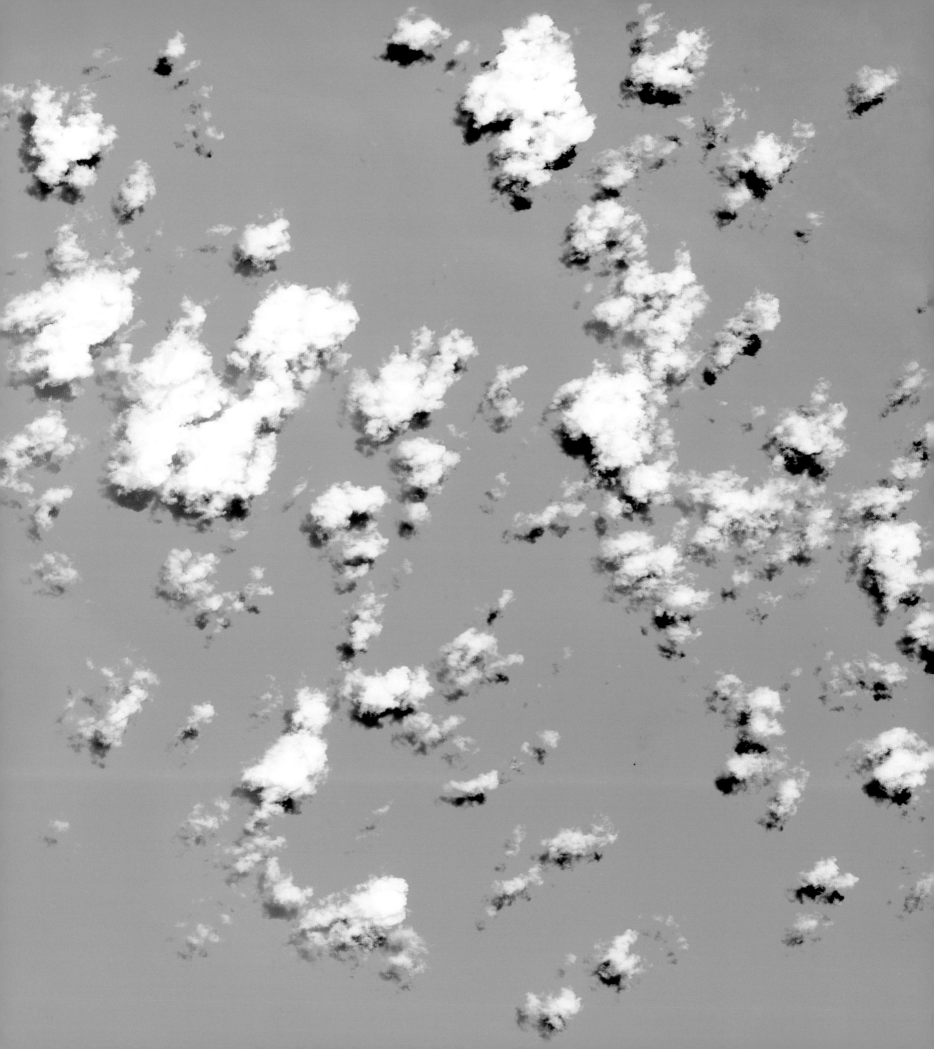

CUMULONIMBUS CLOUDS ↑

Clouds are beautiful examples of Earth's ever-changing weather. Cumulonimbus clouds, like these over Nigeria in western Africa, rise to dramatic heights, sometimes up to 50,000 feet (15,000 m)—higher than passenger planes fly. They are rain clouds, usually delivering powerful downpours. These are also the clouds that produce lightning and hail.

← CUMULUS CLOUDS

These cumulus clouds over the Bahamas in the western Atlantic Ocean are sunny-day clouds, usually no higher than 6,600 feet (2,000 m) above the planet. Normally, cumulus clouds produce little or no rain, but they can grow into the precipitation-bearing cumulonimbus clouds shown above.

ICE MELTING IN UUMMANNAQ FJORD

The Uummannaq Fjord is where eleven ice-sheet glaciers flow into the ocean on the central coast of west Greenland. Every winter, seasonal temperature changes cause snow to pile up and pack together to become ice. During the warmer months of summer, some of the ice melts, and the ends of the glaciers calve (break off) into the water. In the past, there was a balance between the amount of ice gained and lost annually. In recent years, however, scientists have observed that record-high air temperatures, plus warming ocean currents, are causing less ice to form and more ice to melt.

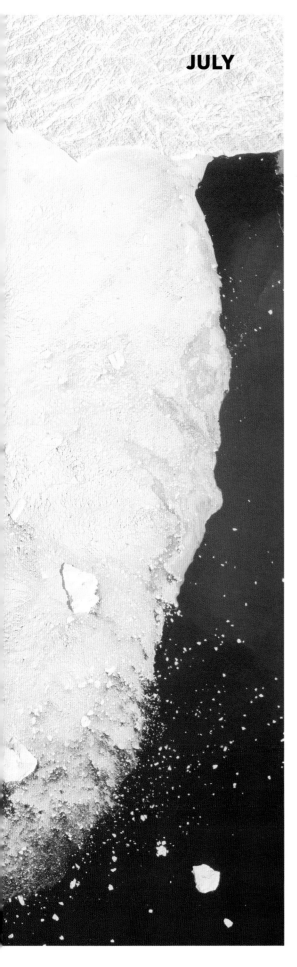

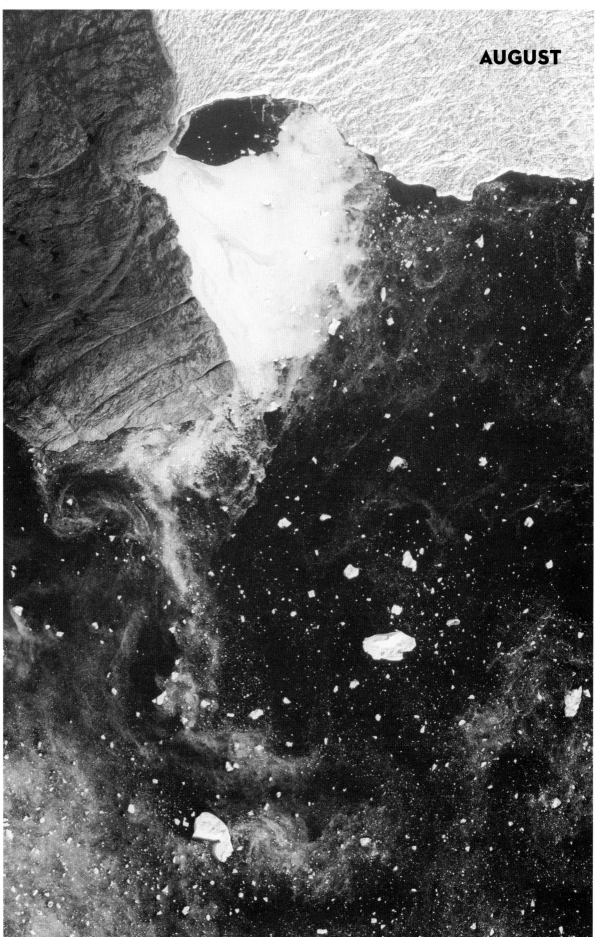

EARTH
COLORS

RED

Lake Natron in Tanzania is so salty, a particular type of cyanobacteria grows there. This bacteria produces a pigment that colors the water a deep red.

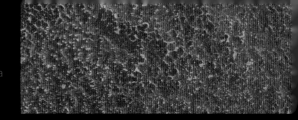

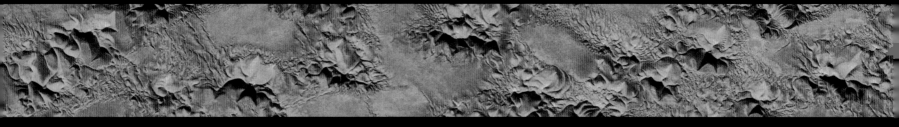

YELLOW

Bright yellow flowering shrubs grow on the Banks Peninsula of New Zealand's South Island.

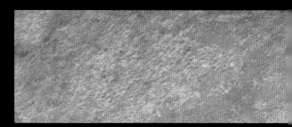

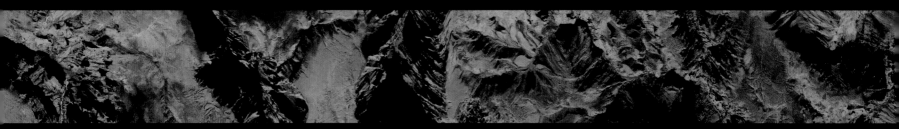

BLUE

This blue is ice-cold! What you see here is a section of the Perito Moreno Glacier in Patagonia, Argentina. The entire frozen field of ice is the world's third-largest reserve of freshwater.

VIOLET

Akimiski Island is an unoccupied piece of land in Canada's James Bay. This purplish color results from a beautiful combination of lichen, moss, and plants called sedges.

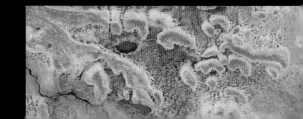

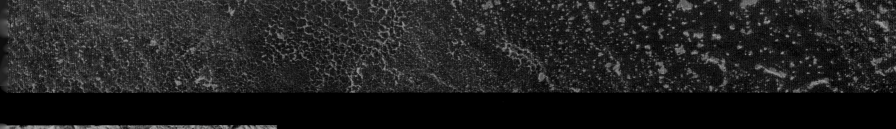

ORANGE

These sand dunes in the Sahara Desert in Algeria are bright orange.
The massive piles of sand receive lots of sunlight and almost no rain.

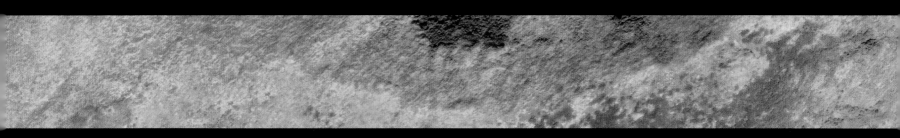

GREEN

Green moss covers the mountainsides in southern Iceland. Much of the
country is made of volcanic rock. Without rich soil, large plants can't take
root—but moss grows all over the place!

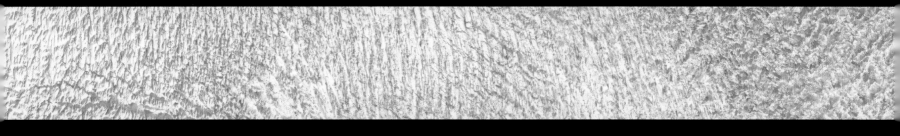

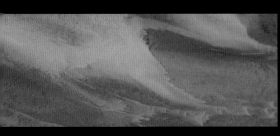

INDIGO

Because there is a shelf of land on the seafloor surrounding the Bahamas,
the depth of the water varies. When seen from space, the lighter blues of
the shallows and the darker blues from the depths result in this amazing
color combination.

CHAPTER 3

A PLANET OF PERIL

Sometimes the effects of natural forces on Earth are catastrophic. Scientists have become better at predicting and warning us about the planet's destructive nature, but it is never easy. Volcanic eruptions can happen unexpectedly, leaving people with no time to get out of the danger zone. Lightning strikes or careless campers can spark powerful wildfires, destroying entire communities and endangering all life in their path. Extremely powerful storms like hurricanes can flood roads and homes, knock out power sources, and cover coastal areas with so much salt water that it takes years before crops can grow on the land again. Scientists predict that with a changing climate, especially one with warmer temperatures, storms like this will happen more often. To better understand the violent side of Earth's nature, this chapter includes several Before and After Overviews that show us the impact of these extreme weather events.

RAUNG VOLCANO

Raung is one of the most active volcanoes on the Indonesian island of Java. In recent decades, it has erupted every few years, most recently in 2015. During that eruption, several airports in Indonesia had to close due to the ash in the air, which made flying difficult. This satellite image, captured with a special infrared camera, shows Raung's 10,932-foot-high (3,332-meter-high) mountaintop crater full of red-hot lava during the 2015 eruption.

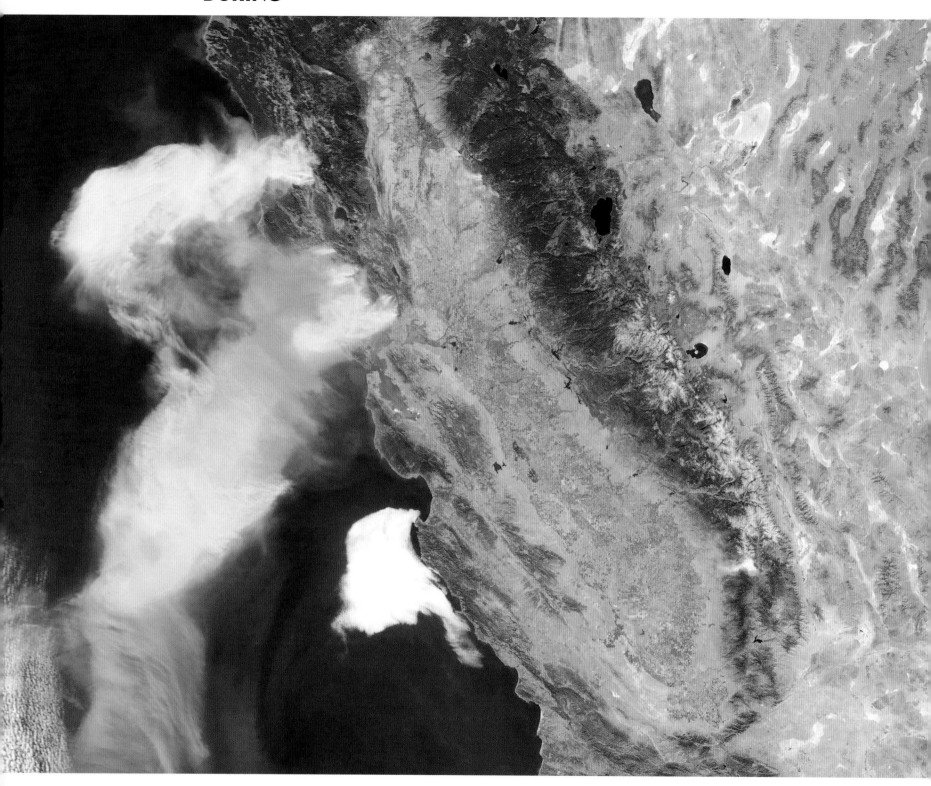

FOREST FIRES IN CALIFORNIA

In October 2017, powerful forest fires broke out near Santa Rosa, California. According to investigators, fires started when strong winds knocked down power lines, causing sparks that ignited dry vegetation. Fanned by these winds, the fires grew and spread rapidly into nearby residential communities, including the neighborhood shown in this Before and After. It is believed that the fires claimed over 6,000 buildings and 42 lives. These deadly and destructive wildfires are a growing danger for California.

DROUGHT IN SOUTH AFRICA

From 2014 to 2018, the city of Cape Town, South Africa, experienced a severe drought. As seen in this Before and After, Theewaterskloof Dam—the city's largest reservoir, which holds nearly half its water supply—was dangerously close to drying up. During the drought, Cape Town residents were subject to strict water rationing, limiting them to

AFTER

no more than 13 gallons (49 l) of water per person per day—about the same amount of water used in a three-minute shower. Thankfully, winter rains that came later in 2018 saved the city from being the first major urban center on Earth to face a "Day Zero"—when the city's water supply would have completely shut off.

FLOODING FROM HURRICANE HARVEY

In late August 2017, Hurricane Harvey crawled across the state of Texas, dumping up to 60 inches (1,524 mm) of rain and causing catastrophic flooding. When the storm was over, it had affected 13 million people across five states, damaging at least 204,000 homes and killing 88 people. By September 1, one-third of the city of Houston was underwater. This Before and After shows some of the flooding in Houston, close to the San Jacinto River.

BEFORE

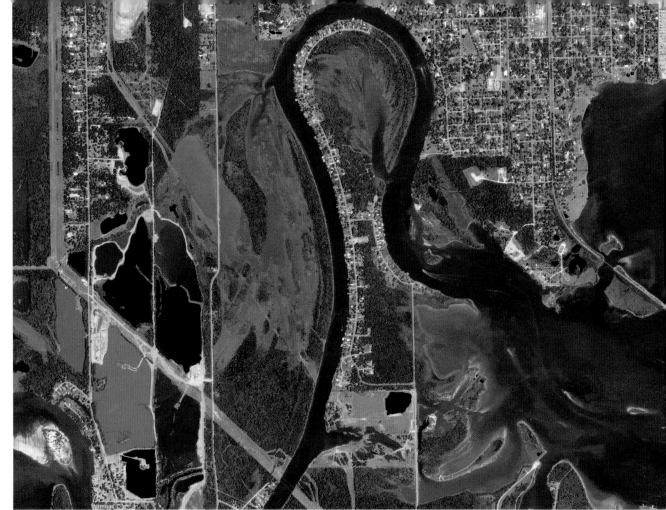

AFTER

BEFORE

DESTRUCTIVE LAVA IN HAWAII

The Kilauea volcano in Hawaii began erupting in early May 2018 and continued into August. Besides flowing lava, white-hot vapor rose from fissures (cracks) in the earth and explosions sent towering columns of ash and lava high into the air over the island. As seen in this Before and After, the eruption destroyed 82 homes and many of the roads in the area known as Leilani Estates. The area remains threatened by possible future eruptions.

(Inset) As seen in the After photo above, the lava from Kilauea flowed all the way into the ocean. When that happens, the ocean water cools the lava, but the heat from the lava boils the seawater and sends steam up into the air.

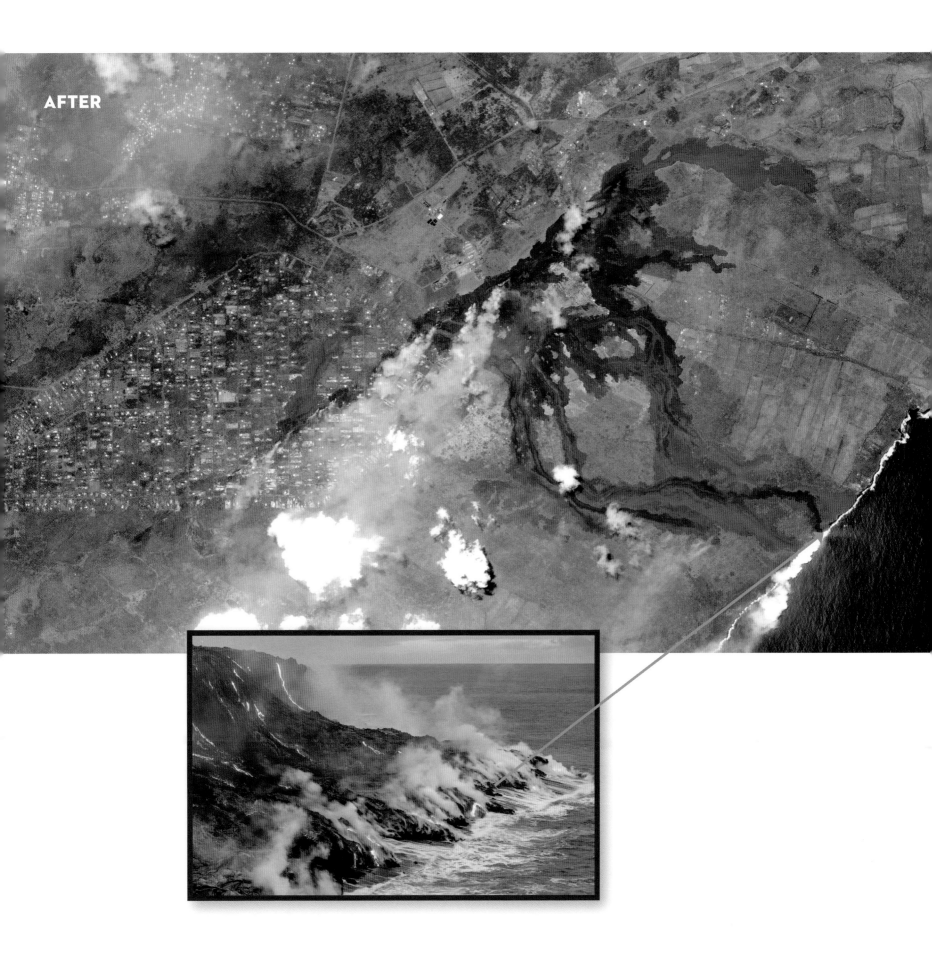

AFTER

PART 2

AN AMAZING EARTH AND US

PALM JUMEIRAH

The Palm Jumeirah is a group of human-made islands that are home to 26,000 people in the city of Dubai, in the United Arab Emirates. These islands were formed on top of land mainly made of rocks and sand brought up from the seafloor of the Persian Gulf. The crescent-shaped outer island is 650 feet (200 m) wide and about 11 miles (18 km) long.

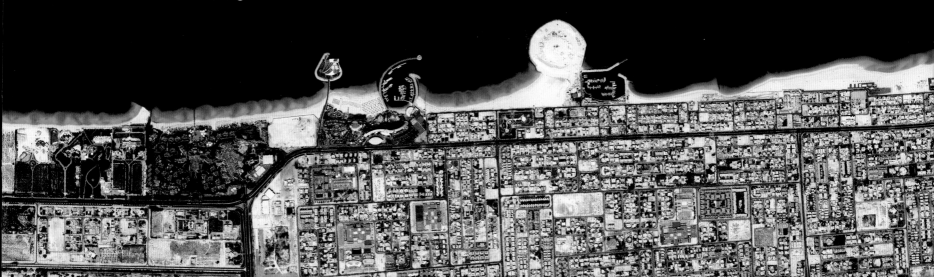

CHAPTER 4

A PLANET THAT FEEDS US

Thousands of years ago, our newfound ability to create a reliable food supply meant humans could stay in one place and devote time to things besides searching for food. It was this invention of agriculture that made modern civilization possible.

In this chapter, you will see stunning examples of how human ingenuity has allowed us to use the land to grow plants and raise animals. From above, the places we harvest often look like woven fabric. With approximately 40 percent of the land on Earth used for agriculture, our ever-growing population—currently 7.5 billion people—challenges us to find more effective ways to feed ourselves.

Advanced farming equipment and powerful chemicals have dramatically increased the amount of crops we can grow and the size of our livestock. People have even created innovative techniques for harvesting the ocean, increasing the global fish catch to six times what it was in the 1950s and cultivating new "crops" in the sea. But problems like a reduced supply of fresh water and severe overfishing force us to think about our future sources. We must be careful not to take more than Earth can spare so we maintain healthy ecosystems that support human life and wildlife side by side.

NILE RIVER

The Nile River flows for 4,132 miles (6,650 km), making it the world's longest river. Every summer, melting snow and heavy rains in the mountains of Ethiopia drain into the Nile. By the time the water reaches Egypt, the river overflows, flooding the flat desert land and turning the banks green with plants all the way to the delta at the river's mouth. Historians believe that this region around the river has been intensively farmed for at least the last 5,000 years.

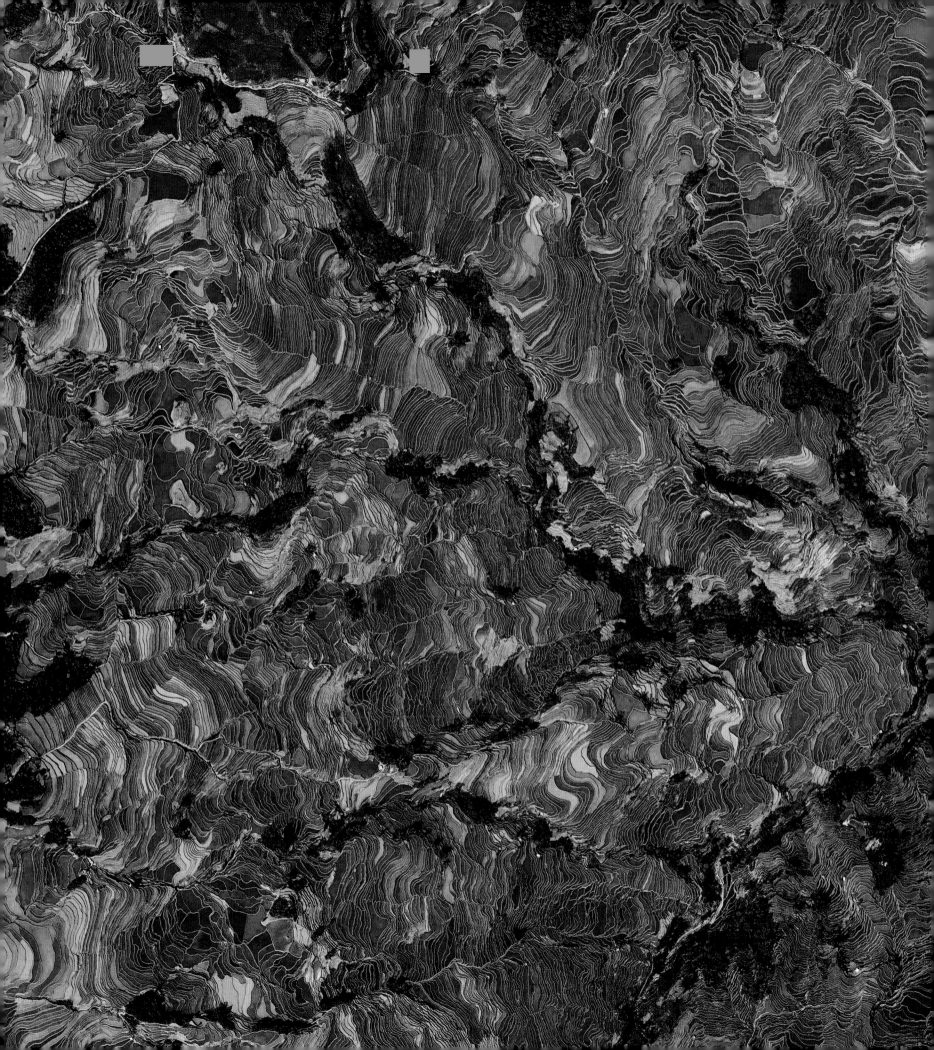

RICE TERRACES

The rice terraces in Yuanyang County, China, include over 3,000 small fields, called steps, that are carved into the sides of mountains. About 2,500 years ago, the Hanai people developed this clever strategy to make farming possible in the hilly region. They also developed a system of channels to bring water from the mountaintops down into the terraces to irrigate the rice growing there.

(Inset) The view across one of the rice terraces shows how they are cut into the hillsides.

CITRUS TREES

Orchards, most likely orange trees, dot the hillsides in Isla Cristina, Spain. The arid climate in this region is ideal for raising citrus crops. Advances in irrigation technology in the 1990s made it possible to plant trees on hillsides where it was previously too steep and dry for anything to grow—leading to larger farms taking root in the area.

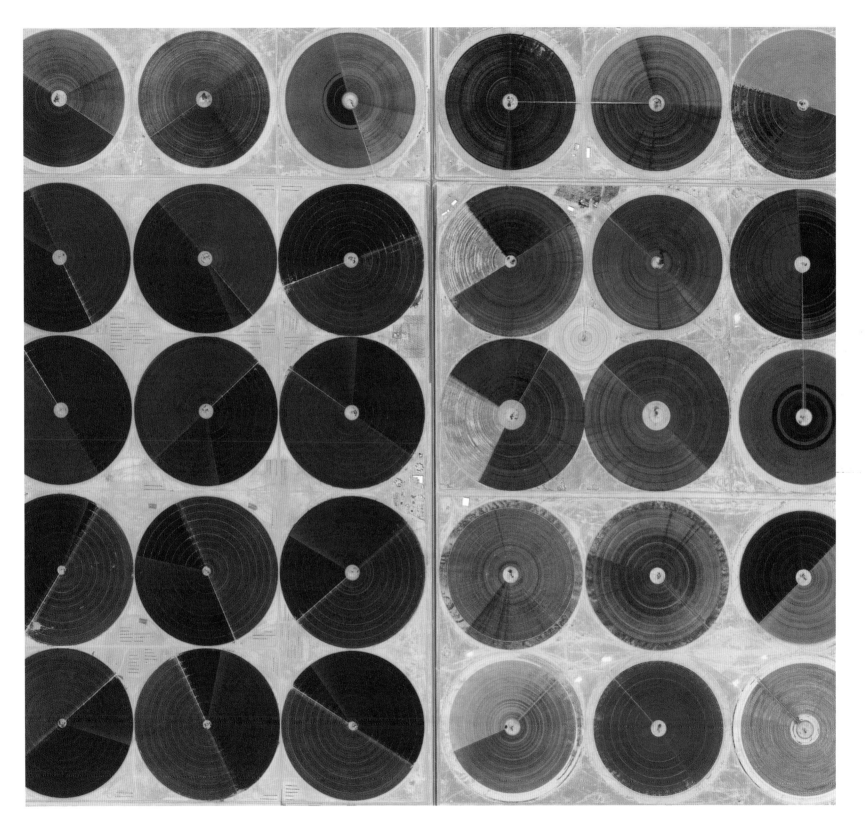

PIVOT IRRIGATION FIELDS

The pivot irrigation fields of Wadi As-Sirhan Basin, Saudi Arabia, show how technology makes it possible for people to grow food even in the desert. Since 1986, water has been pumped from deep beneath the ground up to the surface, and sprayed out of rotating sprinklers. Because the sprinklers revolve around a central motor—a system known as pivot irrigation—they form perfect green circles of crops. Fruits, vegetables, and wheat are grown in the fields here.

AQUACULTURE

Seafood farms cover the surface of Luoyuan Bay in southeastern China. Under the water is a vast network of lines, cages, and nets, where seafood species like crabs, lobsters, scallops, and carp grow. They are protected there until they are large enough for commercial sales. This Overview shows approximately 2.3 square miles (6 square km)—about twice the size of Central Park in New York City.

(Inset) An aerial view shows a few of these farms, surrounded by their cages, built on top of the water.

CATTLE FEEDLOT

What look like tiny dots are actually cows in a feedlot in Summerfield, Texas. Once the cows weigh 650 pounds (295 kg), they are brought here to be fed a special diet of hay supplemented with corn, soy, and other ingredients before they are shipped off to slaughter. That food helps the animals quickly gain weight—as much as 400 pounds (180 kg) in just three to four months! The red area at the top of the feedlot is a pond. The bright color comes from algae growing in the water, which is polluted by the manure (animal waste) that runs off the feedlots.

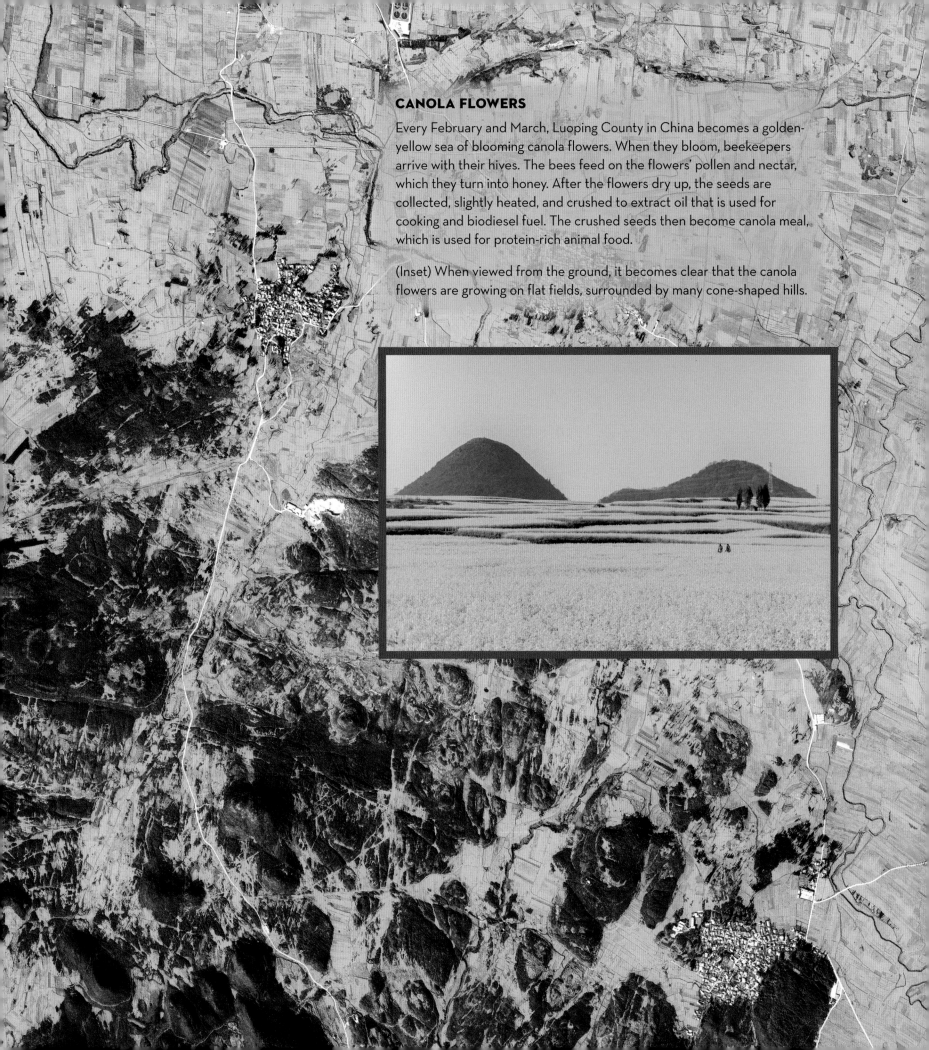

CANOLA FLOWERS

Every February and March, Luoping County in China becomes a golden-yellow sea of blooming canola flowers. When they bloom, beekeepers arrive with their hives. The bees feed on the flowers' pollen and nectar, which they turn into honey. After the flowers dry up, the seeds are collected, slightly heated, and crushed to extract oil that is used for cooking and biodiesel fuel. The crushed seeds then become canola meal, which is used for protein-rich animal food.

(Inset) When viewed from the ground, it becomes clear that the canola flowers are growing on flat fields, surrounded by many cone-shaped hills.

BEFORE
MARCH

TULIPS

Each year from April to late May, the fields around Lisse, Netherlands, transform into multicolored stripes of blooming tulips. As seen in the Before picture, the fields are a lot less colorful in the months before the flowers bloom. The Dutch produce 4.3 billion tulip bulbs each year, of which 2.3 billion are grown for cut flowers. The rest of the bulbs are sold around the world, to be planted and bloom elsewhere.

AFTER
APRIL

CHAPTER 5

A PLANET WE CALL HOME

Looking at the places where we live from above can be powerful and revealing. We can compare different living conditions around the world—some places are hot, and some places are freezing cold. We can tell that some places are wealthy, and some are poor. Some places are crowded, and others are sparsely populated. We can see the hometowns of the people who will be affected most by climate change, built in the areas closest to sea level. We can even observe how much light each city gives off at night.

In the past, urban areas grew without much planning, sprawling outward to make space for houses, roads, and parking lots. New cities are being built from the ground up and carefully planned. Today, urban planning is more important than ever because most of the people on Earth live in cities, from smaller ones of 500,000 people or fewer to megacities with populations of 10 to 20 million. The United Nations estimates that by 2050, two out of every three people will live in a city. We can learn from what we see from space and build cities that not only meet the needs of their citizens, but also minimize the strain they put on the planet.

IPANEMA

Ipanema is a neighborhood in the Brazilian city of Rio de Janeiro. The area is best known for its beach of the same name, which is divided into sections by lifeguard towers, called *postos* (posts). This Overview shows that many people love to live as close to nature as they can.

← JOHANNESBURG

Many studies show a connection between the wealth of a residential area and the trees and green space that it has. More green often means more money. This Overview is a rare example where two places of very different levels of wealth are so close together. In South Africa's wealthy Bloubosrand neighborhood (on the bottom of the image), tree-lined roads are bordered by luxury homes on large lots, many with swimming pools. And just across the street, the impoverished Kya Sands neighborhood has shacks crammed together along paths that drain filthy water from a nearby creek.

DELHI →

With 18.6 million people living in Delhi, India, it's the fifth most populated city in the world. Poorer neighborhoods, such as Santosh Park, have almost no green space, as seen in this densely populated area with no parks and very few trees.

BRØNDBY HAVEBY →

Brøndby Haveby is a residential community outside Copenhagen, Denmark, featuring circular housing areas with cul-de-sacs in the centers. Each house has a pie slice of land with a large green space in the front. This gives the circles a village-like feel, and every homeowner has enough space for a garden to grow their own food.

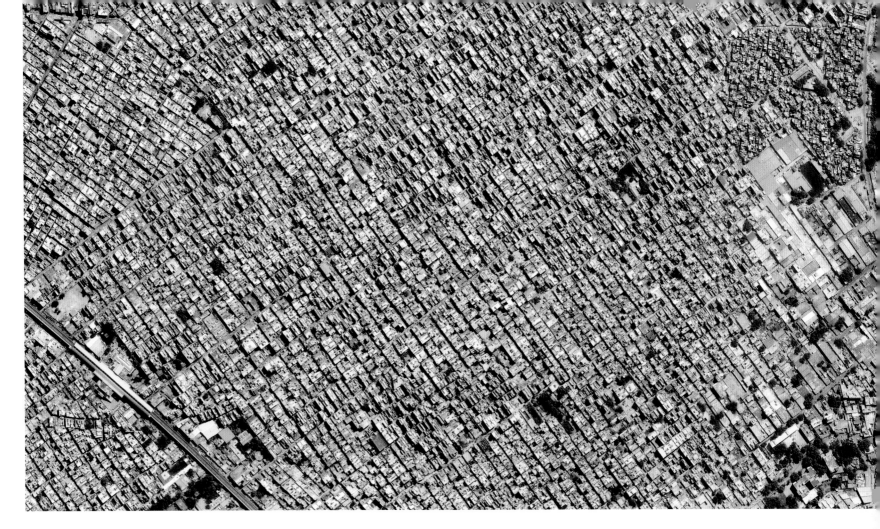

← LONGYEARBYEN

Longyearbyen on the Svalbard Islands of Norway is the world's northernmost town with a population of more than a thousand people. At this remote site, the temperature barely climbs above freezing during the summer and dips as low as –22° Fahrenheit (–30° C) during the winter. The town was founded in 1906 by an American, John Longyear, as the home for the employees of his Arctic Coal Company and their families.

MARABE AL DHAFRA →

Marabe Al Dhafra in Abu Dhabi, United Arab Emirates, is a very hot place to live. In fact, during the hottest season—May through September—temperatures regularly soar as high as 109° Fahrenheit (43° C)! The community is home to roughly 2,000 residents, who are mainly workers at nearby oil and gas production facilities and their families. While the neighborhood finally got its first gas station in 2017, residents must travel 12 miles (20 km) to buy groceries and other supplies.

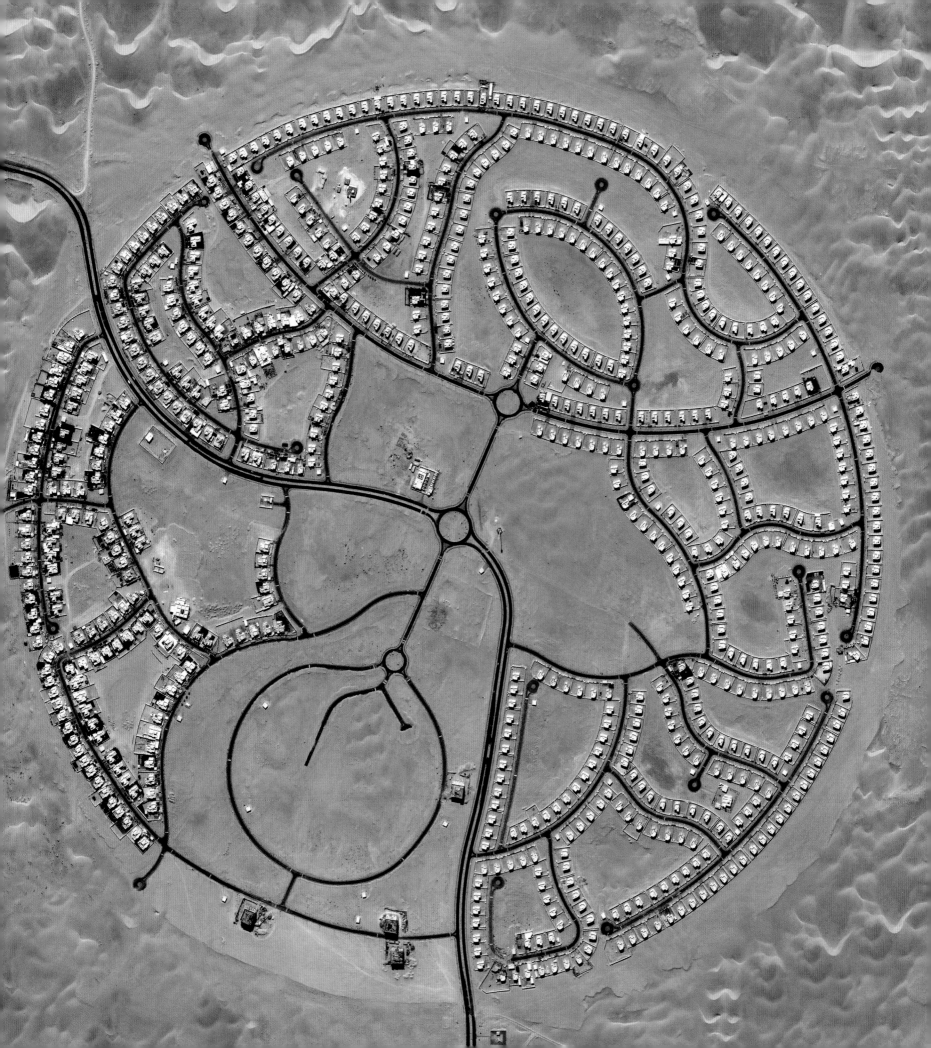

VENICE

Venice, Italy, is built on 118 small islands separated by canals and joined by so many bridges that it is nicknamed the City of Bridges. While its many waterways make Venice uniquely beautiful, they also put the city at risk of flooding. Scientists estimate that the Mediterranean Sea will rise up to 5 feet (1.5 m) by the year 2100. To protect the city, massive floodgates have been built at all three of the Venetian Lagoon's inlets to create a temporary wall against rising sea levels. But according to engineer Paola Malanotte-Rizzoli, due to difficulties with funding, the panels have been installed but can't be raised yet.

MALÉ

Malé is the capital and largest city of the Republic of Maldives, a country of 1,190 islands in the Indian Ocean. Holding the title of "flattest country in the world," about 80 percent of the Maldives is only about 3 feet (0.9 m) above sea level. That lack of elevation means the possibility of rising sea levels is a very serious concern in Malé, which is home to more than 130,000 people—all living within roughly 2 square miles (5.1 square km). So many people in such a small area makes Malé the fifth most densely populated island in the world.

PARIS

The street plan and distinctive appearance of Paris, France, are largely due to the public works program commissioned by Emperor Napoléon II and designed by Georges-Eugène Haussmann. Between 1853 and 1879, Haussmann's team demolished crowded and unhealthy medieval neighborhoods and built a sewer system, parks, public squares, and wide, tree-lined diagonal avenues across the city. This distinct street pattern in the upper left that looks like a star from above is called Place de l'Étoile (*Star's Plaza* in French).

CITIES AT NIGHT

LONDON— Population: 8,800,000

Viewed from space, the bright lights of London, England, reveal how the city is built around the River Thames, which winds through it like a snake.

TOKYO— Population: 9,300,000

Tokyo, the capital of Japan, has more colorful neon signs than any other city in the world. Winter nights also sparkle with stunning displays of LED lights—from displays on buildings to the trees along the Meguro River, where pink lights mimic springtime cherry blossoms.

ISTANBUL— Population: 15,000,000

The lights of Istanbul, Turkey, are divided in two by the city's central waterway, the Bosporus strait, which connects the Mediterranean Sea and the Black Sea.

CHICAGO— Population: 2,700,000

The city of Chicago, Illinois, is easy to spot at night because its tightly gridded streets outline the edge of the very dark Lake Michigan.

CHAPTER 6

A PLANET WE TRAVEL

Once humans started settling down in villages and towns, they needed to find ways to connect with other places. What began as horses, wagons, and small boats has become cars, trucks, trains, planes, and ships that transport people and goods all around the globe. These advancements required footpaths, dirt roads, and small waterways to be developed into paved roads, highways, railroads, ocean sea lanes, and flight paths. These faster modes of travel have made our world feel smaller and more connected.

The massive hubs and intersections that connect us—the network of places where we come together before we head off in separate directions—can be seen from space. Transportation links us to new places and new cultures. It's an important building block of our civilization, one that is becoming more global.

Yet all our moving and hauling impacts Earth greatly, as we pave over land, cut down trees, interfere with wildlife, and release carbon emissions from many of our vehicles. Even the vehicles and parts themselves wear out and need to be recycled so they don't become waste. Perhaps the same innovative spirit that led to such far-reaching human movement can produce new modes of transportation that will help us sustain a healthy planet.

SCHOOL BUS FACTORY

School buses are built at an assembly plant in Tulsa, Oklahoma. Since 1939, laws have required the exterior of most buses to be painted a highly visible yellow. Recently, buses used in locations where it gets hot have been given white roofs. White paint reflects sunlight and has been found to lower interior bus temperatures by as much as ten degrees.

CAR FACTORY

Cars are parked next to the Hyundai factory in Montgomery, Alabama. The plant can produce 300,000 automobiles every year and also contains the production facility for their engines. In 2018, there were about 276 million vehicles registered in the United States. Of those, about 44 percent were cars.

TIRE GRAVEYARD

The world's largest tire dump is in Hudson, Colorado. The facility contains 50-foot (15-meter) pits and has been filled with as many as 60 million used tires. An estimated 1.5 billion tires are discarded each year worldwide. So what do you do with a mountain of waste tires? In some places, they have been burned for fuel, but that practice is being stopped because it's extremely harmful for the environment. Some tires are being shredded and added to asphalt paving and cement used in construction. This more eco-friendly option has been found to reduce cracking in the cement.

THE NARDÒ RING ↑

The Nardò Ring is an 8-mile (13-km) high-speed test track for cars in Nardò, Italy. Built by Fiat in 1975, it is now owned by Porsche and also used by other automobile manufacturers. The usual speed limit for this track is 149 miles per hour (240 kmph). However, clients that arrange for exclusive use of the track can drive at even higher speeds.

← LOMBARD STREET

Lombard Street in San Francisco, California, is known as the "most crooked street in the world." Surprisingly, it began as a straight cobblestone street, but once automobiles became popular, it proved to be too steep. When the street was paved in 1922, eight hairpin turns were added in the one-block section seen here to make it safe to drive on.

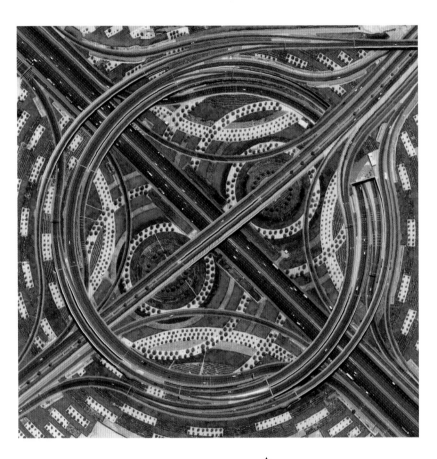

WHIRLPOOL INTERCHANGE ↑

An interchange is the place where two or more highways come together. This interchange near the Miracle Garden in Dubai, United Arab Emirates, is called a whirlpool interchange because of its circular, intertwined highways and on-off ramps that cross over a straight twelve-lane highway.

TURBINE INTERCHANGE ↑

A turbine interchange connects two highways in Jacksonville, Florida. The wide curves of the roads make for an easy flow of heavy traffic. However, the large amount of land required to build an interchange like this makes them uncommon.

INMAN TRAIN YARD

Inman Yard handles most of the railroad traffic into and out of Atlanta, Georgia. It is run by Norfolk Southern, a major transporter of coal that operates 20,000 miles (32,187 km) of track in 22 states and the District of Columbia. They also maintain one of the largest fleets of railroad cars in North America, with 72,560 freight cars— including more than 21,000 coal cars and 4,073 locomotives.

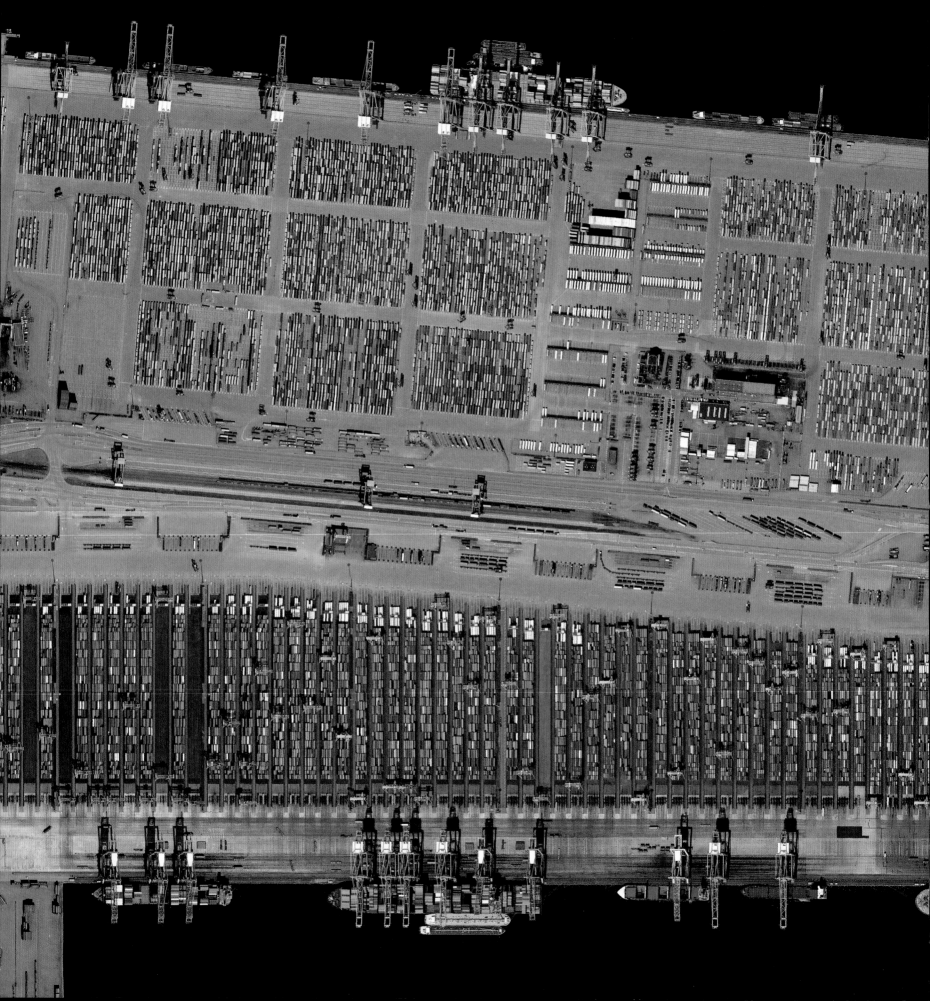

PORT OF ROTTERDAM

The Port of Rotterdam in the Netherlands was the world's busiest port from 1962 to 2004. Though it lost that title first to Singapore and then to Shanghai, China, it is still the largest port in Europe. The massive docked container ships seen here weigh up to 300,000 tons (272,000 metric tons) and extend up to 1,200 feet (366 m)! Each of those tiny multicolored rectangles is a 20-foot-by-9-foot (6 m by 3 m) metal container full of goods that are being shipped somewhere in the world.

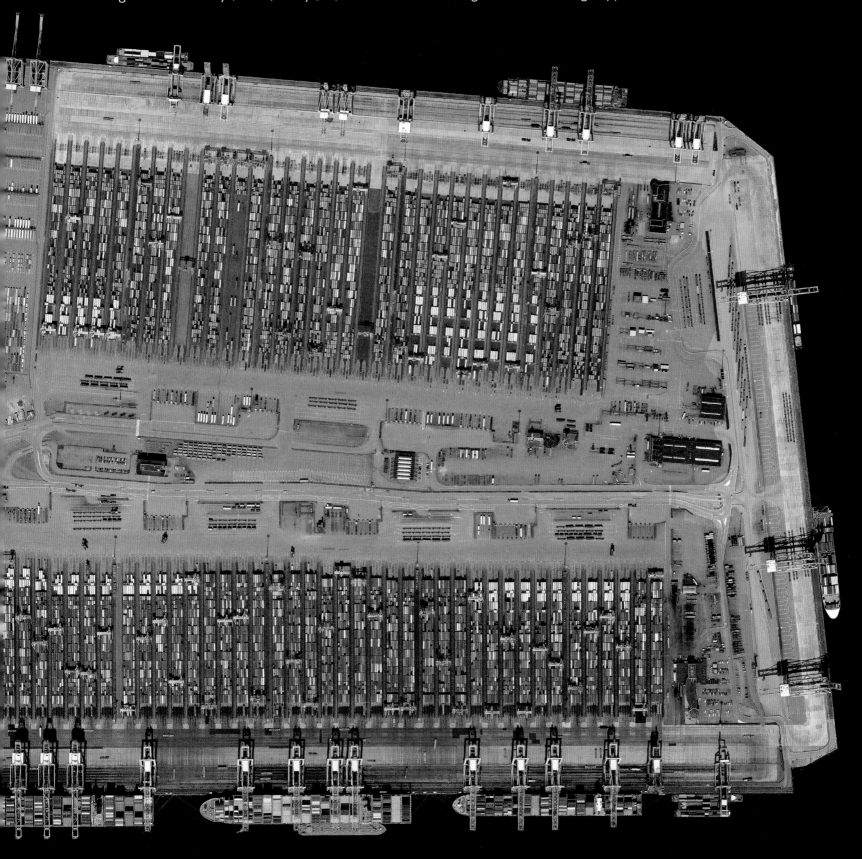

← PORT OF SINGAPORE

Cargo ships and tanker ships often have to wait to enter the Port of Singapore. The port is so busy that one ship enters or leaves every two to three minutes and about a thousand ships are docked there at any one time. It is no wonder, then, that the Port of Singapore has been either the first or second busiest container port in the world since 2005. One of the reasons this port is so busy is that it is well equipped and deep enough to handle some of the world's biggest ships.

SHIPBREAKING YARD →

Chittagong Shipbreaking Yard, located on an 11-mile (18-km) strip on the Bay of Bengal in Bangladesh, is one of the world's largest shipbreaking centers. More than 200,000 workers use blowtorches, sledgehammers, and metal cutters to break up ships to recycle the steel and other metals. The facility recycles as many as 230 ships per year. Breaking down a single ship by hand can take months, but so many are taken apart at Chittagong because the labor is cheap. However, the unsafe working conditions—use of dangerous machinery and exposure to toxic chemicals—lead to many injuries, even deaths. In 2018, a bill was passed to protect the workers and punish companies that fail to protect them. Hopefully, this will improve the lives of the workers soon.

AIRPLANE FACTORY

The Boeing factory in Everett, Washington, is the world's largest manufacturing facility. The main assembly building is so big, it could hold 75 football fields! Boeing's 28,000 employees have the use of 450 adult tricycles to quickly get around the huge facility. The massive open layout of the building makes it possible to construct mammoth passenger jets indoors.

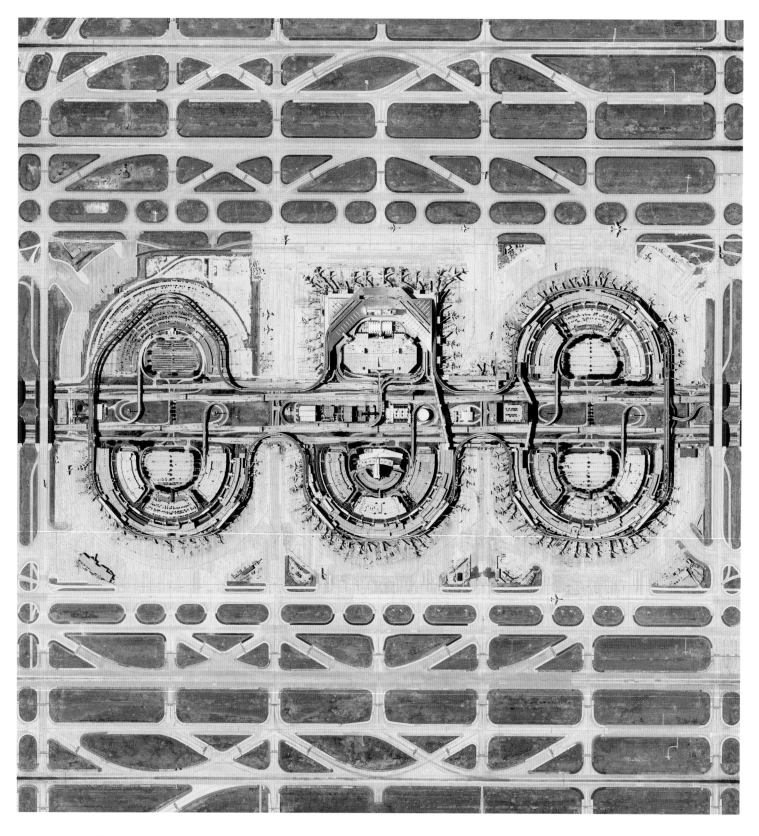

DALLAS FORT WORTH INTERNATIONAL AIRPORT

Dallas Fort Worth International Airport stretches across 30 square miles (77 square km), making it larger than the island of Manhattan. In 2017, this airport was the twelfth busiest airport in the world measured by passenger traffic, with 64 million travelers passing through it every year.

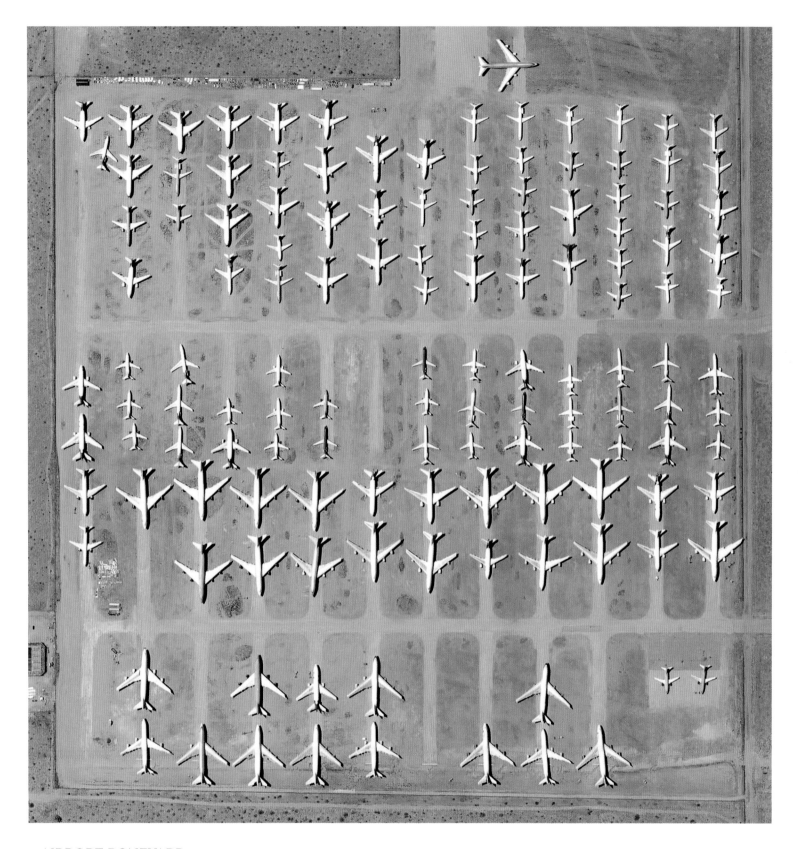

AIRPORT BONEYARD

The Southern California Logistics Airport boneyard in Victorville, California, is a storage site for about 300 retired airplanes. Located in the Mojave Desert, the warm, dry climate is perfect for preserving these planes for many years. While they wait, the planes are given special care: windows are covered with aluminum foil, all fluids are drained, and the engines are removed. The planes then become sources for valuable parts, such as electronics and scrap metal.

CHAPTER 7

A PLANET THAT PROVIDES FOR US

Almost everything we do requires energy. It lights our homes, powers our cell phones and video games, fuels our cars, and cooks our food. To get that energy, we dig, pump, strip, and frack, using whatever methods we have invented to extract the raw materials we need from our planet. These resources are then shipped around the world to be refined, processed, and made usable.

The places we mine are some of the most visible human-made landmarks from space. It is fascinating to see where the raw ingredients for the things we buy come from. Yet digging and stripping Earth leaves scars and artificial colors rarely seen anywhere else. When we take fossil fuels from underground and burn them for energy, we release carbon dioxide into the atmosphere, contributing to poor air quality and climate change. And the waste left behind after these products are used presents even more problems for our planet.

The resources on the following pages are not unlimited, and our ability to make up for the damage caused by our widespread use also has its limits. We need to shift to energy sources that are renewable and less damaging to the planet—such as wind and solar power—while also using less of everything else. The future of Earth is in our hands.

COAL TERMINAL

The Qinhuangdao Coal Terminal in China is the world's largest coal-shipping facility. From here, approximately 210 million tons (190 million metric tons) of coal are transported to power plants throughout southern China each year. China's coal-burning power plants produce about 70 percent of the country's electricity.

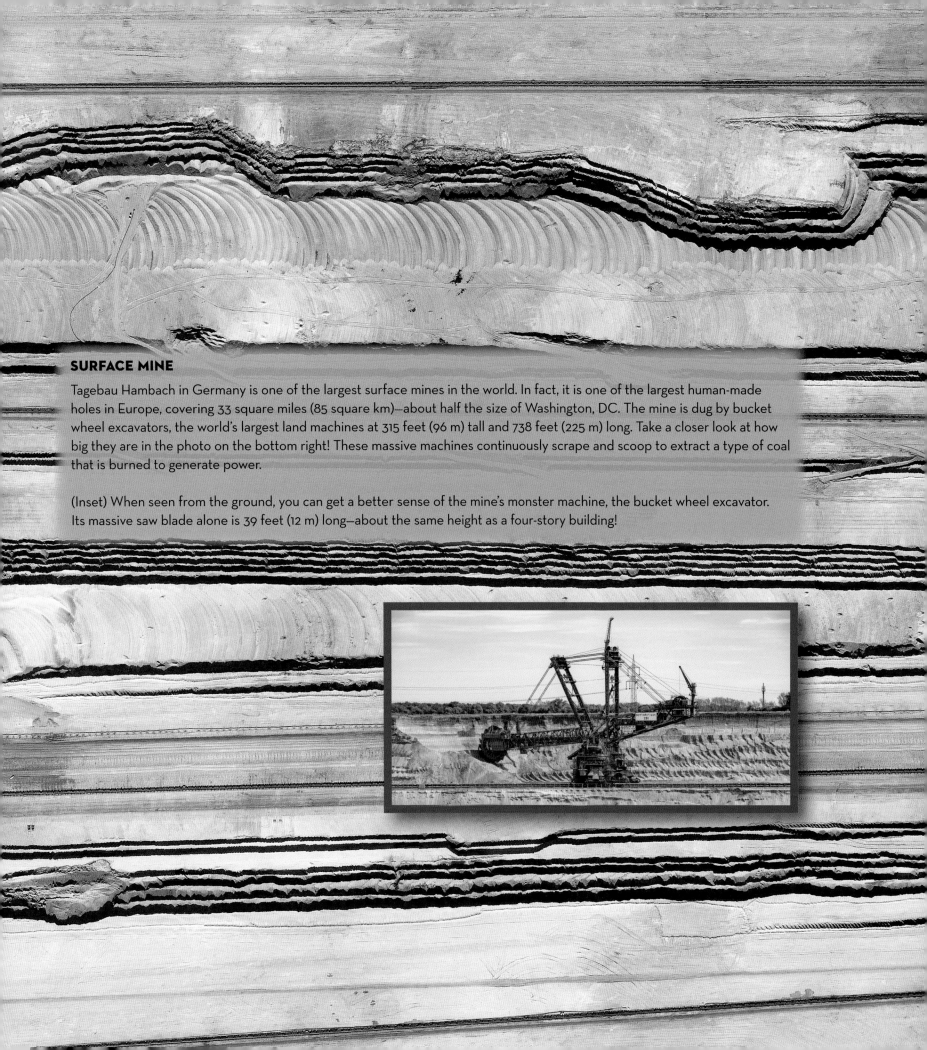

SURFACE MINE

Tagebau Hambach in Germany is one of the largest surface mines in the world. In fact, it is one of the largest human-made holes in Europe, covering 33 square miles (85 square km)—about half the size of Washington, DC. The mine is dug by bucket wheel excavators, the world's largest land machines at 315 feet (96 m) tall and 738 feet (225 m) long. Take a closer look at how big they are in the photo on the bottom right! These massive machines continuously scrape and scoop to extract a type of coal that is burned to generate power.

(Inset) When seen from the ground, you can get a better sense of the mine's monster machine, the bucket wheel excavator. Its massive saw blade alone is 39 feet (12 m) long—about the same height as a four-story building!

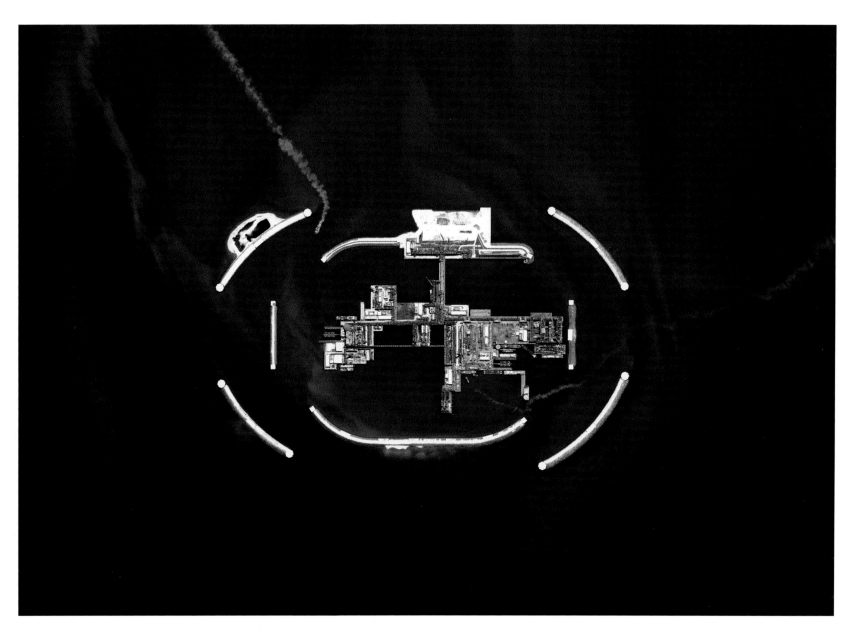

OIL PLATFORM ↑

The Kashagan Oil Platform is in the Caspian Sea near Kazakhstan. The giant structure pumps oil from the Kashagan Reservoir, about 13,780 feet (4,200 m) below the seafloor. Building the pumping facility took thirteen years because of frigid winter temperatures and thick ice that covers the sea part of the year. Then, just three months after it opened, a pipeline leak delayed oil production for three years. Once it was reopened in 2018, the platform reported it was producing 300,000 barrels of oil per day.

OIL RIG →

The Prirazlomnoye oil rig in Russia's Pechora Sea is an ice-resistant, weather-hardy rig. Covering 1,356 square feet (126 square m) at the surface, it's anchored to the seabed and has thick walls surrounding the wells to protect the seawater from contamination. Environmentalists remain concerned that an oil spill would seriously damage this Arctic region, but the oilfield's projected reserve of more than 610 million barrels of oil make it too valuable a resource to leave untapped.

OIL REFINERY

The Ulsan Oil Refinery in South Korea is the third-largest in the world. An oil refinery removes impurities from crude oil that is pumped from the ground. The crude oil arrives in Ulsan in tanker ships from the Middle East, South America, Africa, and the United States. Once the crude oil is cleaned, it can be used as gas in cars, diesel fuel, and jet fuel.

DIAMOND MINE ↑

The Mir Mine in Mirny, Russia, now closed, had an output of 10 million carats (4,400 pounds) of diamonds per year during its peak in the 1960s and is still the second-largest excavated hole in the world at 1,722 feet (525 m) deep and 3,900 feet (1,200 m) wide. Diamonds are used for jewelry and industrially for cutting, grinding, and drilling.

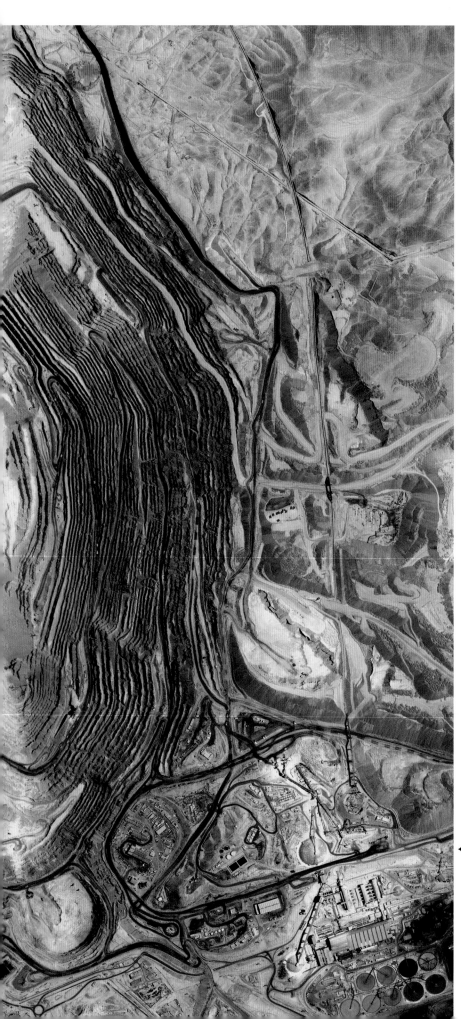

← COPPER MINE

More than 29 million tons (26 million metric tons) of copper have come out of the Chuquicamata mine north of Santiago, Chile, since it opened in 1910. Copper is used in electrical wires, roofing, plumbing, and industrial machinery.

URANIUM MINE ↑

The Arlit uranium mine in Niger extracts and sends uranium to France, where it generates energy in nuclear power plants and is used in the production of nuclear weapons.

LITHIUM MINE →

At the Soquimich mine in northern Chile's Atacama Desert, lithium is collected in human-made evaporation ponds. It is used to make lithium batteries for technology like electric cars, cell phones, and hover boards, and also to make medicine.

IRON ORE MINE

The Mount Whaleback iron ore mine in Western Australia produces more than 30 million tons (27 million metric tons) of ore per year. Roughly 98 percent of that iron ore is used to make steel, which is then used to construct buildings and manufacture items such as automobiles, refrigerators, and swing sets.

(Zoom circle) For a sense of scale, these two blue trucks are each 50 feet (15 m) long.

ZOOM

SAN FRANCISCO BAY SALT PONDS

These salt production ponds are located in San Francisco Bay in California—over 16,500 acres (6,677 hectares). Here's how it works: First, saltwater from the bay is pumped into these massive ponds. Then warm air and wind blowing over the surface evaporates the water, leaving the salt behind. The salt is then scraped out of the ponds and used for many things, primarily cooking. The varied colors of the ponds are a result of different microorganisms (tiny living things) that make their home in water with varying levels of salt.

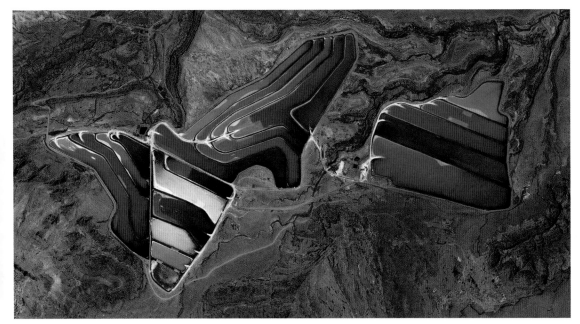

POTASH SOLAR EVAPORATION PONDS

Near Moab, Utah, potash production takes place in solar evaporation ponds. Potash—a type of salt used primarily in crop fertilizers—is located deep underground in pools of very salty water called brines. This water is pumped to the surface and into the ponds. There, the hot, dry desert air evaporates the water. The pools are dyed dark blue to speed up evaporation because blue water absorbs more light and evaporates faster. As seen in this series of photographs, that color fades over time. In total, it takes about 300 days before the water completely evaporates and the potash can be harvested.

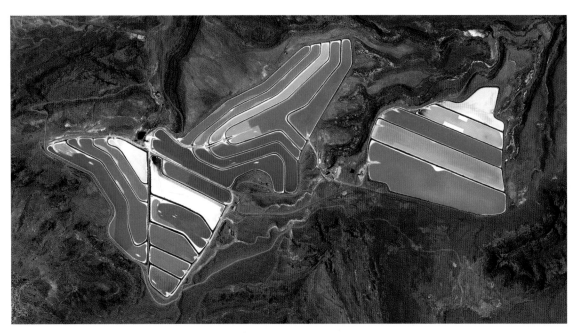

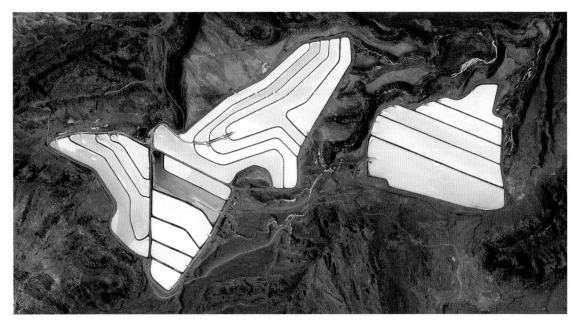

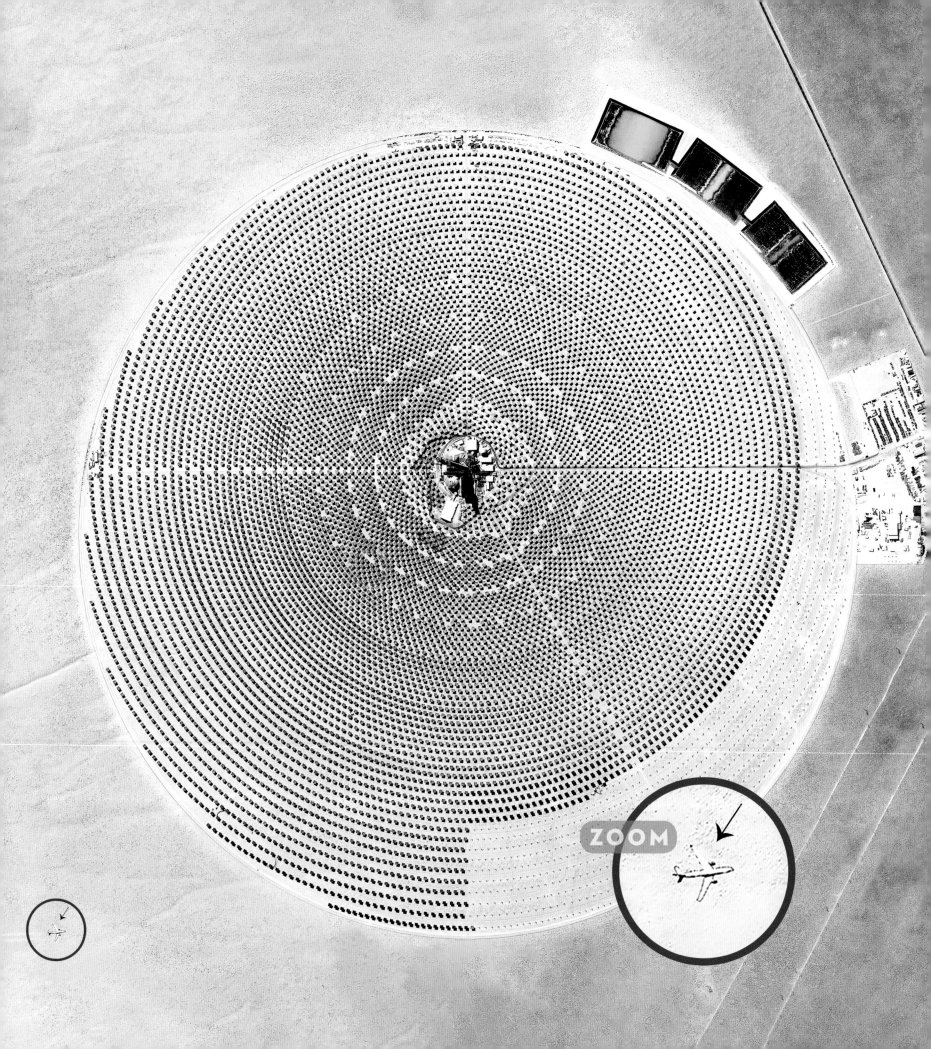

ZOOM

SOLAR ENERGY PROJECT

← **SOLAR ENERGY PROJECT**

Seen here during its construction, the Crescent Dunes solar power plant in Tonopah, Nevada, is the first commercial power plant in the world to generate electricity using molten salt, heated by the sun. Here's how it works: All the 10,347 special mirrors reflect sunlight toward the top of the central tower, which contains hot liquid salt. That concentrated solar energy makes the salt very hot, which then becomes the heat source, instead of coal or oil, to change the water in a generator to steam and produce electricity—enough to power 75,000 homes. To get a sense of how big this facility is, check out the large commercial airplane flying over the complex, enlarged in the zoom circle on the right.

SOLAR PANDAS →

Panda Green Energy Group decided to highlight the benefits of solar power by building a 50-megawatt solar farm in the shape of two panda cubs in Datong, China. Each panda is made of black or gray film solar cells. When completed, the solar farm will contain four pandas and will deliver power to more than 10,000 homes. Fun fact: The idea to build the solar farm in the shape of pandas didn't come from the company that built it, but from a local teenager!

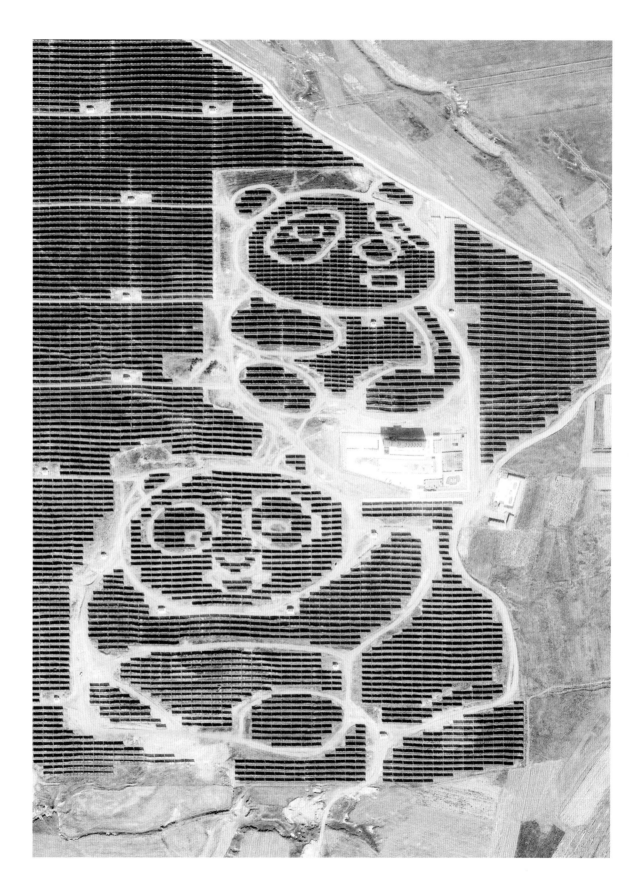

OFFSHORE WIND FARM

The Donghai Bridge wind farm in Shanghai, China, is the country's first large offshore wind farm (meaning it is built out in the sea) and has the capacity to power 200,000 homes. The "streamers" trailing from each wind turbine are actually sediment in the water. This shows how the turbines are influencing the sea's natural currents. Researchers have also discovered some plants and animals living at the base of the turbines.

(Inset) These wind turbine towers are 299 feet (91 m) tall, and the blades have a diameter of 295 feet (90 m).

SHILOH WIND POWER PLANT

The Shiloh wind power plant covers the Montezuma Hills of California. The facility includes 275 turbines spread out over 6,800 acres (2,750 hectares). Local farmers, who lease space on their land to build the turbines, use the surrounding area for sheep grazing and growing hay.

CHAPTER 8

A PLANET WE CHANGE

While natural disasters can destroy parts of Earth, the planet is also greatly impacted by humans. With all the ways we are drastically changing the planet—like the trash we send to landfills or the carbon dioxide we pump into the atmosphere—we are using and destroying air, water, and soil resources so quickly, Earth may never be able to replace them.

Pollutants are speeding up climate change, creating years with average temperatures that are hotter than ever before, affecting where plants can grow and where animals can live. Large areas of the planet's forests have been cut down. And rising temperatures, oil spills, and plastic waste dumped in the oceans have all been very harmful to aquatic life.

The results of many of these serious human-made changes can be seen in the Overviews in the next pages. They have the power to show us how connected we are to Earth. Every time we use up, waste, or destroy resources, we damage our home planet for every living thing, now and in the future.

IRON ORE MINE WASTE POND

Lake Gribben on the Upper Peninsula of Michigan is so polluted that it is stained bright pink. The source of this pollution is the waste and by-products generated by iron ore mining at a site nearby. Due to these toxins, environmental agencies warn that it is unsafe to eat any fish caught in this lake. For a sense of scale, this Overview shows approximately 1 square mile (2.6 square km) of the polluted water.

DEFORESTATION IN BRAZIL ↑

The Amazon is the world's largest tropical rain forest. Unfortunately, an area roughly as large as the country of France has been cut down to harvest logs, clear land for farming and cattle ranching, and build towns. In this Overview, you can see how loggers are clear-cutting trees alongside major roads. It is vital to save what remains of the rain forest. Its trees and plants not only produce the oxygen that people and animals need to survive, but they also remove some of the Earth-warming carbon dioxide from the atmosphere. Rain forests are also home to thousands of amazing species of plants and animals that live nowhere else in the world.

DEFORESTATION IN BOLIVIA →

Deforestation is visible in Santa Cruz, Bolivia, right next to untouched healthy areas of rain forest. Bolivia is one of the poorest countries in the Western Hemisphere and has struggled with a difficult decision—protect its precious forest or cut down trees to sell for timber, clear the land to plant crops, or open it to drilling for oil and gas. Between 2000 and 2014, an estimated 4.5 million acres (1.8 million hectares) of rain forest were lost in Bolivia. Scientists predict that all of Bolivia's rain forest may be turned into grassland and farmland by 2100 if the current rates of clearing continue.

MISCHIEF REEF

Mischief Reef in the South China Sea is one of seven coral reefs that China has turned into an artificial island. In 2015, China sent dozens of dredging ships to the reef. They used sand from the ocean floor, rocks, and cement to build up the reef, creating land above the surface of the water but killing the coral and animals living around the reef in the process.

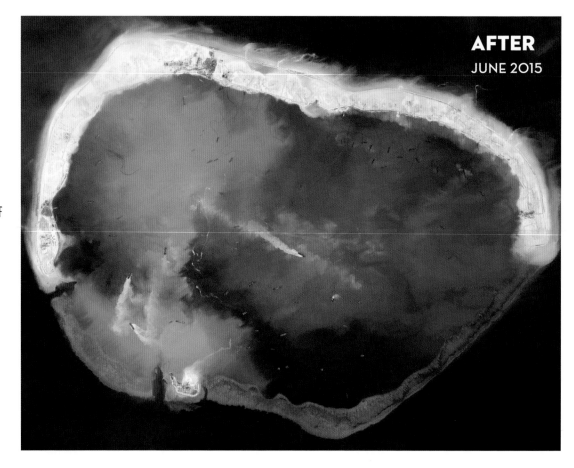

AFTER
JUNE 2015

The Before and After Overviews show the changes there in just six months. China claimed this island was necessary to hold lighthouses to help ships safely navigate through the area. But then they built an airplane landing strip (not shown in these photos), causing international concern over what their real plans for Mischief Reef might be.

SUDOKWON LANDFILL

Even our garbage can be seen from space! At least it can when it is in one of the world's largest dumps—Sudokwon Landfill in Incheon, South Korea. Nearly all the waste from millions of homes in South Korea's capital city, Seoul, and its suburbs ends up at this 570-acre (231-hectare) landfill. In 2017 alone, 230,000 truckloads of waste were dumped here. One section is full, and a golf course was built on top of it in 2012. The area around the active section is smelly, thanks to the methane gas released by the decaying garbage.

DAM COLLAPSE

On November 5, 2015, a dam at an iron ore mine in Brazil collapsed, releasing a toxic tidal wave. Poisonous wastewater raced downstream, flooding many villages like Bento Rodrigues, shown in these Before and After Overviews.

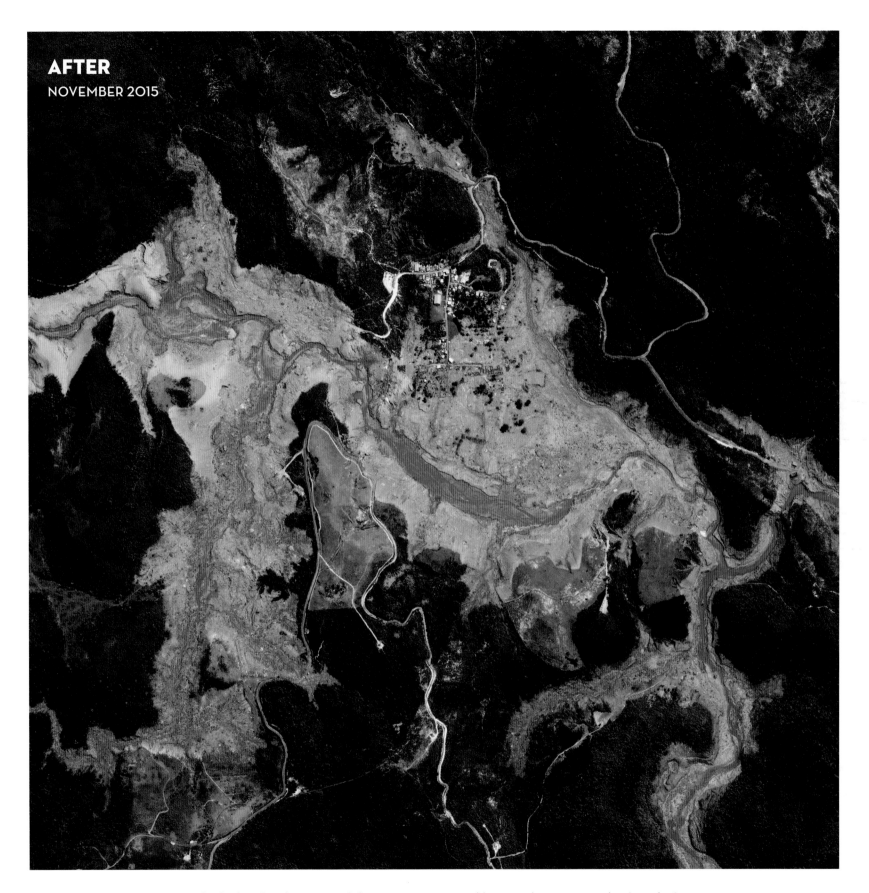

Nineteen people died in this disaster, and the mining waste quickly spread across 311 miles (500 km), destroying the land, polluting the water, and killing many plants and animals. Cleanup to make this town livable again is estimated to continue for a decade, but nobody knows how long it will take for the area to fully recover.

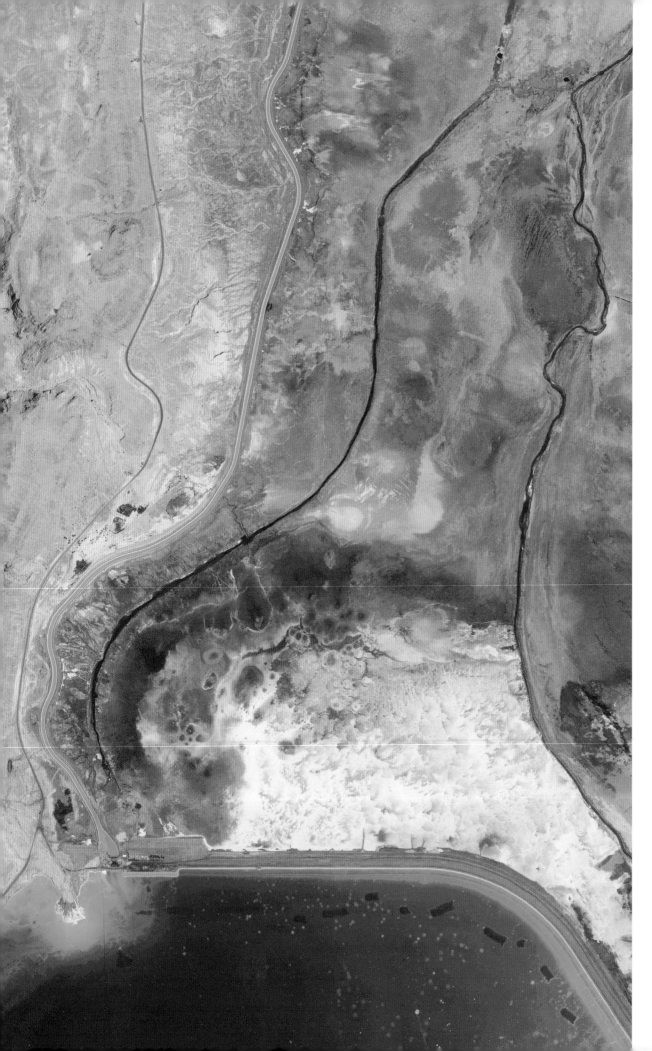

THE SHRINKING DEAD SEA

The Dead Sea in the Jordan Rift Valley (between Jordan and Israel) is one of Earth's saltiest bodies of water—9.6 times saltier than the oceans! And the water is getting saltier because the water level in the lake is dropping by more than 3 feet (0.9 m) per year. In the past, the Dead Sea maintained a fragile balance, gaining fresh water from mountain rivers and streams to offset what was lost through evaporation. Then surrounding countries began diverting the water to help supply their populations with water. In 2013, Israel and Jordan signed an agreement to build a pipeline to transport water from the Red Sea across the desert to the Dead Sea, but as of 2018, the cost and difficulty of carrying out this project has put it on hold.

MADAGASCAR EROSION

Madagascar, an island in the Indian Ocean off the east coast of Africa, looks as though it is bleeding at the Betsiboka River delta. This coloring is actually from all the soil that washes off the land when it rains— more than 180 tons (163 metric tons) per acre each year. The erosion is getting worse as the country's native forest is cut down to clear land for farming, leaving the soil more exposed. When the soil is lost, the area is less able to support plant growth. But the erosion also has an impact downstream, where the soil is deposited. Soil buildup has made Bombetoka Bay more shallow, so large ships entering the bay are now in danger of running aground.

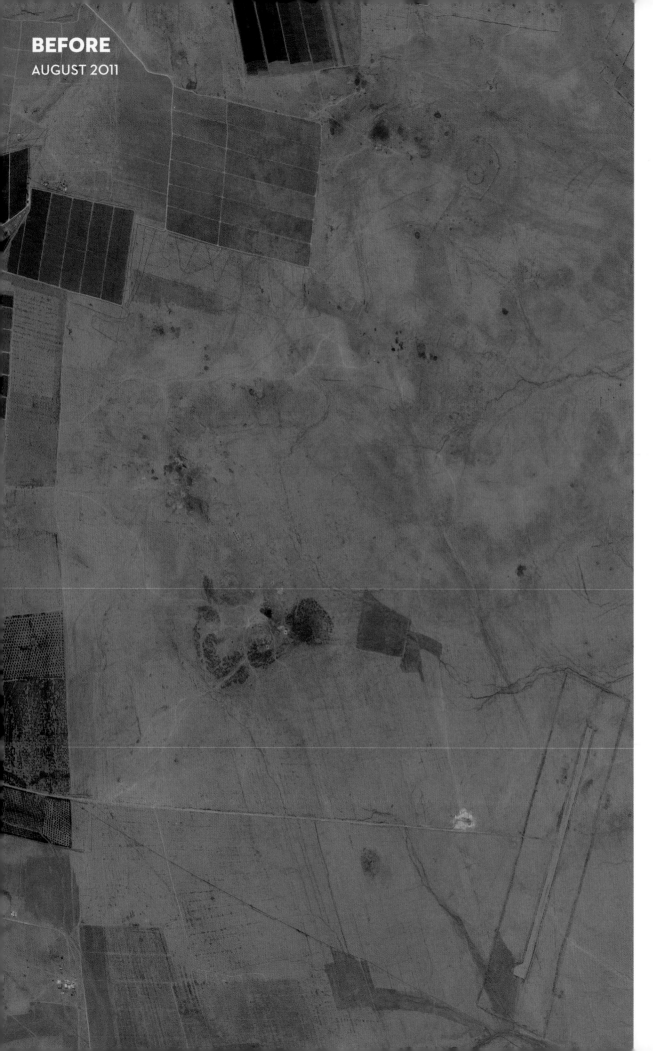

ZAATARI REFUGEE CAMP

Zaatari Camp, close to Mafraq, Jordan, has become the largest refugee camp for Syrians displaced by the ongoing Syrian civil war. When first established in 2012, it was only a small tent camp. By 2018, it had become a more permanent settlement of around 80,000 people spread over about 2 square miles (5.2 square km). It now has schools, shops, and electricity from a solar power plant.

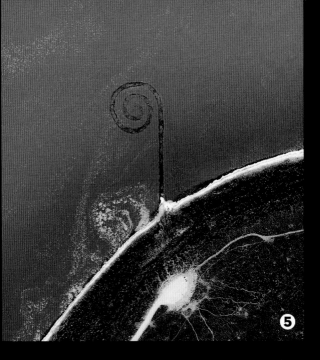

5

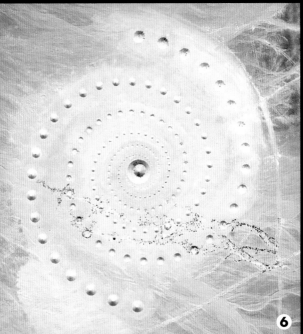

6

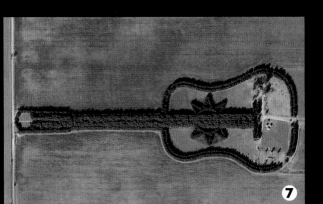

7

EARTH
SHAPES

1. CIRCLE—MOUNT TARANAKI

The land around this active stratovolcano on the west coast of New Zealand is a circular protected forest. There is a very noticeable change in vegetation between the darker green forest and the lighter green of the dairy farms that surround it.

2. TRIANGLE—LUKE AUXILIARY #4 RUNWAY

This abandoned airfield outside of Phoenix, Arizona, was closed at some point between 1956 and 1966, but its triangular runways are still visible in the desert.

3. PENTAGON—THE PENTAGON

The Pentagon is the headquarters of the United States Department of Defense, located in Arlington County, Virginia. The building has five sides, five floors above ground, and five ringed corridors on each floor, with a combined length of 17.5 miles (28 km).

4. STAR—PALMANOVA

The medieval town of Palmanova, Italy, is surrounded by a star-shaped fort designed so an attack on any wall could be defended from the two closest star points, allowing soldiers to fire at the intruder from the front and rear.

5. SPIRAL—SPIRAL JETTY

This sculpture by Robert Smithson is a 1,500-foot (457-m) spiral jutting into the Great Salt Lake in Utah. Smithson reportedly chose this site because of the vibrant colors of the water, caused by the bacteria and algae that live there.

6. DOUBLE SPIRAL—DESERT BREATH

This work of art in the Egyptian desert covers an area of about 1 million square feet (92,900 square m). One spiral is made of 89 cones dug into the ground. The other spiral is formed by using that dug-up sand to create 89 cones raised above the ground.

7. GUITAR—GUITAR FOREST

This unique human-made forest in Argentina is made of 7,000 cypress and

CHAPTER 9

A PLANET OF MARVELS

Throughout this book, we have seen how humans have changed the planet as we have grown and spread out across the globe. While some of those changes have been harmful, we have also created many breathtaking structures and buildings along the way. Humans have always been hard at work, using their creativity to construct places so special, we are awestruck in their presence. And viewing these human-made wonders from above can reveal splendor and spectacle that is not apparent from ground level.

In some instances, the material of the building is the most amazing part, such as the intricate sandstone blocks that were linked together to construct the temple of Angkor Wat in Cambodia. Others, like the Palace of Versailles in France, are known for their elegance and grandeur. And perhaps the most ambitious exist as a combination of necessity, innovation, and awesomeness, like the Golden Gate Bridge in San Francisco.

All of these places showcase the best of human ingenuity and creation. And because we are forever innovating and constructing, there are bound to be new creations that we will add to these lists of marvels in the future. Maybe you could be the one to imagine, design, and build Earth's next great wonder!

SYDNEY OPERA HOUSE

The Sydney Opera House is known for its famous "shell" design that appears white from a distance but actually features a pattern of two different-color tiles: glossy white and matte cream! The building hosts more than 1,500 shows each year in its various performance halls, drawing a total audience of approximately 1.2 million people.

← ANGKOR WAT

Angkor Wat in Cambodia is one of the world's largest religious monuments and was built in the twelfth century as a Hindu temple. As seen in this Overview, the 500-acre (208-hectare) site features a moat and a forest that surround a massive temple at its center. The main temple area alone is four times the size of Rome's Vatican City. And it is constructed of massive sandstone blocks joined without any cementing mortar.

THE PYRAMIDS OF GIZA →

The pyramids of Giza are located on the outskirts of Cairo, Egypt. Dating back to 2580 BC, the Great Pyramid is the largest of the three pyramids at the site and is the only one of the Seven Wonders of the Ancient World to remain intact. The 481-foot (147-m) pyramid was the tallest structure in the world for more than 3,800 years. Experts believe it took 20,000 to 30,000 laborers at least twenty years to build all the structures. Oddly enough, the super-strong mortar that holds those stones together has been studied, but no one has yet been able to re-create it!

THE PALACE AND GARDENS OF VERSAILLES

The Palace of Versailles, outlined in red on the left side of this Overview, is located just outside of Paris, France. The building is considered an architectural work of art, with 700 rooms that give the palace nearly 700,000 square feet (65,000 square m) of living space.

The gardens of Versailles, which take up most of this Overview, cover 1,977 acres (800 hectares) and include 200,000 trees and 210,000 flowers, 50 fountains, 620 water jets, and a Grand Canal—seen in the center— where the king's visitors used to row in Venetian gondolas.

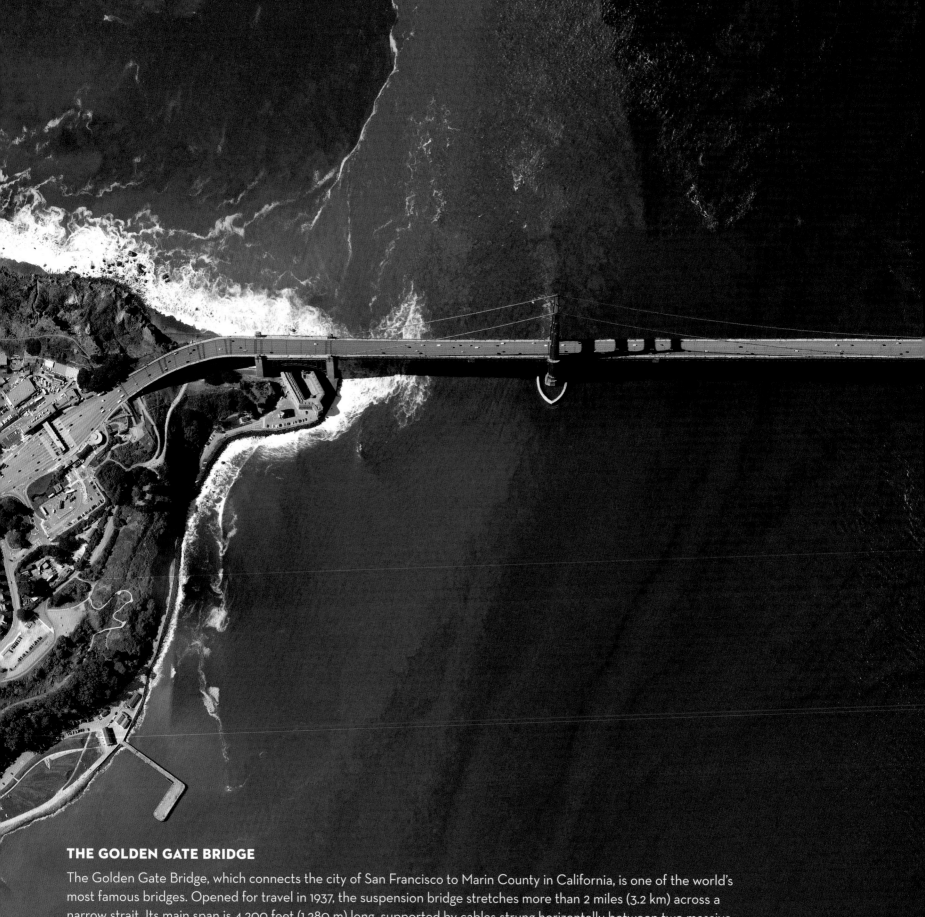

THE GOLDEN GATE BRIDGE

The Golden Gate Bridge, which connects the city of San Francisco to Marin County in California, is one of the world's most famous bridges. Opened for travel in 1937, the suspension bridge stretches more than 2 miles (3.2 km) across a narrow strait. Its main span is 4,200 feet (1,280 m) long, supported by cables strung horizontally between two massive concrete blocks on each side. The bridge, which took four years to construct, is painted a famous "international orange" color that helps it stand out in the fog that often surrounds it.

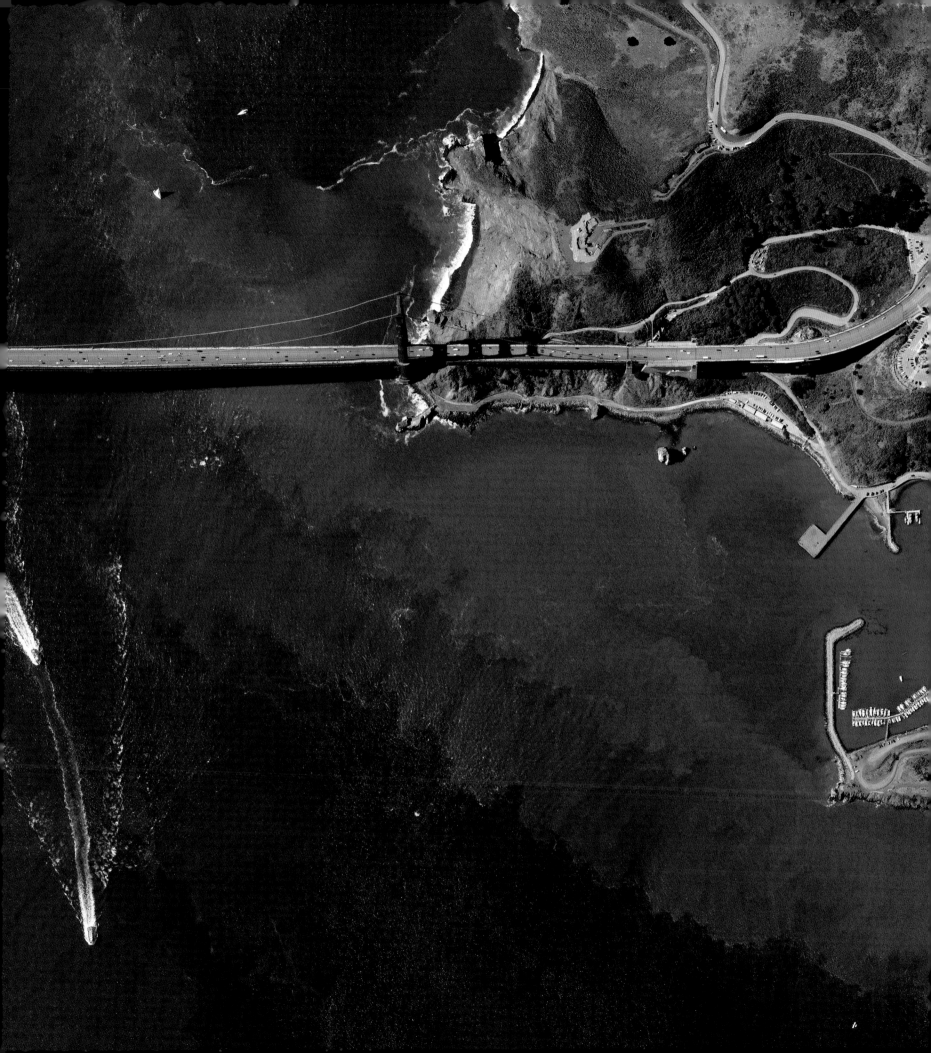

← THE STATUE OF LIBERTY

The Statue of Liberty, which stands in the harbor of New York City, was a gift from France to the United States to celebrate the friendship between the two countries during the American Revolution. The statue was built out of copper by the sculptor Frédéric-Auguste Bartholdi, then separated into 350 pieces and shipped to New York in 214 crates. Putting the statue back together took four months. Lady Liberty stands upon a star-shaped granite pedestal and is visited by more than 4 million tourists every year.

HOOVER DAM ↑

The Hoover Dam on the Arizona-Nevada border was built to harness the Colorado River in order to generate hydroelectric power and supply fresh water to the surrounding areas. Construction on the dam began in 1930 and was finished in 1935. In total, about 3.3 million cubic yards (2.5 million cubic m) of concrete was used to build a massive 726-foot-tall (221-m-tall) dam—enough to pave a road from New York City to San Francisco! The water that filled the canyon behind the dam was named Lake Mead and is now the largest reservoir in the United States.

CENTRAL PARK

Central Park in New York City is one of the most famous parks in the world and was America's first landscaped public park. In 1853, the city bought more than 750 swampy, rocky acres (304 hectares) in the center of Manhattan that were unsuitable for building homes and businesses. Next, a landscape design contest was held to choose Central Park's overall plan. The winner was Frederick Law Olmsted. Soon 20,000 workers dug and shaped the land so that 270,000 trees and shrubs could be planted. Central Park first opened to the public in the winter of 1859.

(Inset) Central Park is located in the middle of Manhattan. The park takes up roughly 6 percent of the island's total area.

WORLD-RECORD HOLDERS

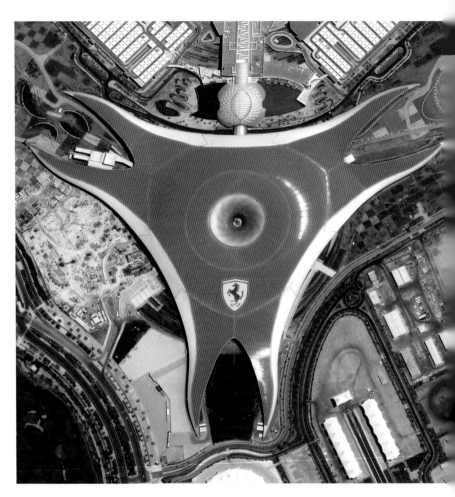

THE WORLD'S LARGEST INDOOR THEME PARK ↑

Ferrari World in Abu Dhabi, United Arab Emirates, is the world's largest indoor theme park. It covers 925,700 square feet (86,000 square m) and contains Formula Rossa—the world's fastest roller coaster.

← **THE WORLD'S TALLEST BUILDING**

The Burj Khalifa in Dubai, United Arab Emirates, is the tallest building in the world, rising 2,717 feet (828 m) into the sky. The design of the 163-floor structure is based on a type of desert flower called the *Hymenocallis,* which has long petals extending from its center.

THE WORLD'S BIGGEST MAZE ↑

The Masone Labyrinth at Fontanellato, Italy, covers 20 acres (8 hectares) and has 2 miles (3.2 km) of internal paths. The maze walls are made of more than 20,000 bamboo plants that rise up to 16 feet (5 m) tall.

THE WORLD'S LONGEST BRIDGE OVER WATER →

The Jiaozhou Bay Bridge—connecting the Chinese city of Qingdao to an island called Huangdao—holds the Guinness World Record for the world's longest bridge over water. And the longest continuous over-water section is 16 miles (26 km) long. That's long enough to span the English Channel with a little room to spare.

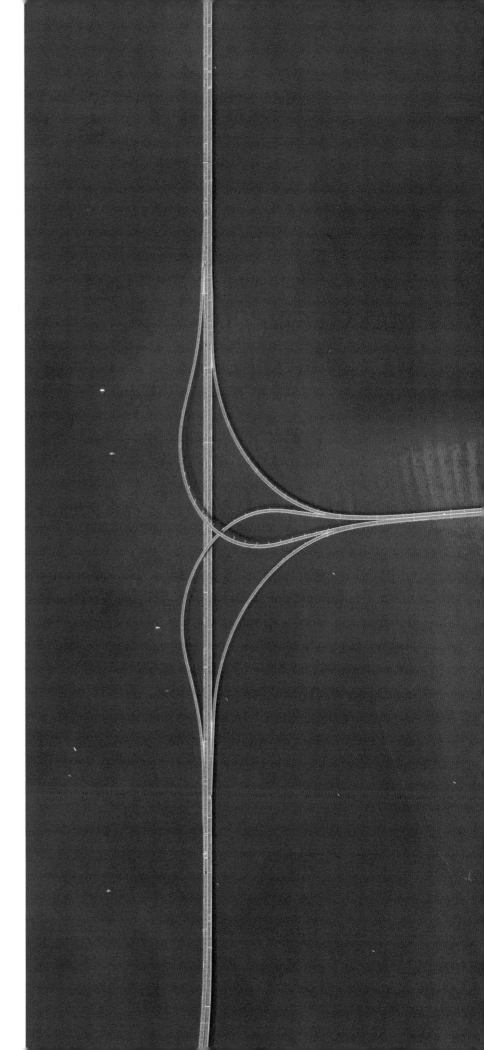

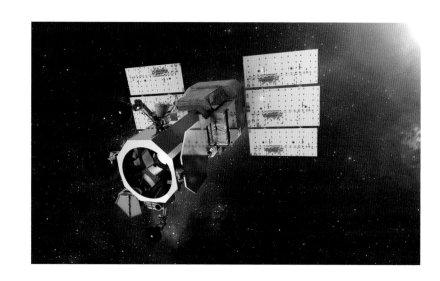

THE TECHNOLOGY THAT MAKES *OVERVIEW* POSSIBLE

MAXAR SATELLITES

Commercial satellite operator Maxar Technologies makes the amazing images in *Overview* possible. The company has four satellites positioned approximately 400 miles (644 km) above the Earth's surface. These satellites are at slightly different heights but all travel along north-south orbits at roughly 17,500 miles (28,163 km) per hour! Each makes about fifteen laps around the Earth every day, completing one orbit every 92 minutes.

With the satellites orbiting so quickly, they do not have much time to snap sharp, clear pictures of any one spot on the surface. But the engineers at Maxar designed the satellite cameras with this in mind. The cameras on board the satellites are *huge*—about 18 feet (5 m) long and about 8 feet (2.4 m) wide, with lenses just under 4 feet (1.2 m) wide. The size of the lens makes it possible to photograph large areas all at once. For example, while passing over Chicago, just one photo can capture the entire city! On top of that, the cameras are so powerful, you can take a clear picture of a basketball from 400 miles (644 km) away!

We are very thankful that our friends at Maxar have let us use their satellites and this incredible technology to see our Earth in a brand-new way.

WORLDVIEW—3 SATELLITE
An artist's rendering shows what the Maxar WorldView-3 Earth-observation satellite looks like in space.

EXPLORE MORE

DAILY OVERVIEW

Started by author Benjamin Grant, Daily Overview lets you see a new picture of our Earth from above each and every day. Also visit the website to buy other books and posters of Overviews.

Instagram: @dailyoverview

Facebook: Daily Overview

Check out these other books and websites to learn more about Earth and how we can protect it for the future.

Barnard, Bryn. *The New Ocean: The Fate of Life in a Changing Sea*. New York: Alfred A. Knopf, 2017. Explore the lives of jellyfish, orcas, sea turtles, tuna, coral, and blue-green algae, and investigate how pollution plus rising water temperatures affect them—and us.

Burns, Loree Griffin. *Life on Surtsey: Iceland's Upstart Island* (Scientists in the Field series). Boston: Houghton Mifflin Harcourt, 2017. Follow the field studies of an Icelandic team investigating the changes of a volcanic island formed by a 1963 eruption.

Cherrix, Amy. *Eye of the Storm: NASA, Drones, and the Race to Crack the Hurricane Code* (Scientists in the Field series). Boston: Houghton Mifflin Harcourt, 2017. Scientists use technology to track hurricanes and monitor their strength to warn people in their projected path.

Delano, Marfé Ferguson. *Earth in the Hot Seat: Bulletins from a Warming World*. Washington, DC: National Geographic Kids, 2009. Explore the dangers and challenges Earth faces as a result of global warming.

Easy Science for Kids: Volcanoes. easyscienceforkids.com/all-about-volcanoes. Check out volcanoes—both their outside and inside structures. Don't miss the action video!

Fleischman, Paul. *Eyes Wide Open: Going Behind the Environmental Headlines*. Somerville, MA: Candlewick, 2014. A group of writers share facts about environmental issues and offer a guide for evaluating news stories and real ways to make a difference.

Goldstone, Bruce. *I See a Pattern Here*. New York: Henry Holt and Co. Books for Young Readers/Macmillan, 2015. Stunning photos let you share nature's artwork and the many diverse patterns found naturally on Earth.

Hopkins, H. Joseph. *The Tree Lady: The True Story of How One Tree-Loving Woman Changed a City Forever*. La Jolla, CA: Beach Lane Books, 2013. Be inspired by this true story of how one woman worked to make a difference for the environment.

Interactive Sites for Education. interactivesites.weebly.com/habitats.html. Lots of fun activities exploring Earth's different habitats.

Kirk, Ellen. *Human Footprint: Everything You Will Eat, Use, Wear, Buy, and Throw Out in Your Lifetime*. Washington, DC: National Geographic Kids, 2011. This is an amazing look at the products you will likely use up in your lifetime.

Markle, Sandra. *The Great Monkey Rescue: Saving the Golden Lion Tamarins*. Minneapolis: Millbrook Press/Lerner Publishing, 2015. Share the excitement of scientists and volunteers from around the globe as they rush to save golden lion tamarins from extinction by planting trees.

NASA Climate Kids. climatekids.nasa.gov/power-up. Discover how wind and water can supply us with electricity. Play games, explore activities, and meet interesting people with exciting careers—maybe one you'd like to share in the future.

Newman, Patricia. *Plastic, Ahoy! Investigating the Great Pacific Garbage Patch*. Minneapolis: Millbrook Press/Lerner Publishing, 2014. Investigate how part of the ocean became swamped with millions—maybe billions—of pieces of plastic trash and what can be done about it.

Newquist, HP. *From Here to There: The Story of How We Transport Ourselves and Everything Else* (Smithsonian Invention & Impact series). New York: Viking, 2017. Explore a timeline that shares modes of travel along the ground, over water, and through the air.

Paul, Miranda. *One Plastic Bag: Isatou Ceesay and the Recycling Women of the Gambia*. Minneapolis: Millbrook Press/Lerner Publishing, 2015. After reading, decide how you can follow this real-life example and make a difference for your community and the planet.

Science For Kids: Waterfalls. scienceforkidsclub.com/waterfalls.html. Explore waterfall basics and learn some amazing facts.

Wagstaffe, Johanna. *Fault Lines: Understanding the Power of Earthquakes*. Victoria, Canada: Orca Book Publishers, 2017. This selection of stories and photos bring earthquakes and tsunamis to life.

HOW YOU CAN HELP

*Explore these books and websites for ways you
can help your home planet to have a healthy future.*

Earth Day: The World's Largest Environmental Movement

earthday.org

Check out the annual events, and make a difference all year long!

The Earth captured by NASA's
DSCVR satellite from 1 million
miles (1,609,344 km) away

Earth Guardians: Protect Our Future

earthguardians.org/pof

Discover how children around the world are working to ensure Earth has the best possible future.

Also, try these seasonal activities you can share.

Earth Rangers

earthrangers.com

Join the team to learn amazing facts about wild animals and tackle challenges that will help them
in their wild homes.

Footprints: Conservation Society

footprintseducation.org/kidz-zone/how-can-i-help.php

Choose your mission and work with your family to protect the Earth. Lots of little efforts can make
a big difference for the planet.

9 Ways Kids Can Protect the Planet

thebarefootmommy.com/2017/04/earth-day-for-kids/

Here are nine ideas to get your family, friends, and community working to protect home base—Earth.

10 Things You Can Do to Save the Ocean

nationalgeographic.com/environment/oceans/take-action
/10-things-you-can-do-to-save-the-ocean

Doing each of these things will help the ocean stay healthy.

INDEX

If you want to explore any of the Overviews in this book in more detail, simply type a set of coordinates seen here into the search bar of Google Earth or the satellite mode of Google Maps!

ACKNOWLEDGMENTS

To my family—thank you for your endless support of me and this project.

To Emily—thank you for believing in this idea and for the guidance that brought it to life.

To Sandra—thank you for contributing so much experience and excitement to this book.

To Trish, Larsson, Nicole, Sam, and the rest of the team at Penguin Random House— thank you for your continued collaboration and belief in my work.

To Tim—thank you for believing in the hypothesis and for your devotion to shaping it with me.

To Pat, Graham, Adam, Peter, Patrick, Katya, and Dylan—thank you for always bringing out my inner child.

To Michelle—thank you for your encouragement to be patient and follow through.

To Kira and Eli—thank you for your teamwork that makes it possible to keep this project going.

To Maxar Technologies, Nearmap, NASA, and Axelspace—thank you for creating the beautiful technology that offers us access to these new perspectives.

And to all the parents who decided to share these images with your children—thank you for inspiring an idea that will hopefully lead to a better home for all the generations to come.

The authors would like to thank the following people for sharing their enthusiasm and expertise: Turner Brinton, Public Relations Manager, Maxar Technologies, Denver, Colorado; Mary Grikas, Vice President of Global Communications, SolarReserve, Santa Monica, California; Dr. Daniel Macfarlane, Assistant Professor of Environment and Sustainability, Western Michigan University, Kalamazoo, Michigan; Dr. Carsten Lemmen, Coastal Research Department, Helmholtz-Zentrum, Leuphana University, Geesthacht, Germany; Dr. George "Pinky" Nelson, NASA Space Shuttle Astronaut, Retired; Shannon Ream, Digital Media Manager, Corporate Communications, Maxar Technologies, Boulder, Colorado; Dr. Paola Malanotte-Rizzoli, Department of Earth, Atmospheric and Planetary Sciences, Massachusetts Institute of Technology, Cambridge, Massachusetts; Dr. Julie Rose, Research Ecologist, NOAA, Northeast Fisheries Science Center, Milford Laboratory, Milford, Connecticut, USA; Dr. Lonnie Thompson, School of Earth Sciences and Byrd Polar Research Center, The Ohio State University, Columbus, Ohio; Dr. Colin D. Woodrooffe, School of Earth and Environmental Sciences, University of Wollongong, Australia